Califa Uhuru

A Compilation of Literature

from

The Moorish Science

Temple of America

This Text is the Property

of

____

Califa Uhuru

Califa Media Publishing ™

Originally published by the
Moorish Science Temple of America

Edited by
Sis. Tauheedah S. Najee-Ullah El

Introduction by
G.S. Rami A. Salaam El

Califa Uhuru

Originally published by the
Moorish Science Temple of America

Edited by
Sis. Tauheedah S. Najee-Ullah El

Introduction by
G.S. Rami A. Salaam El

TABLE OF CONTENTS

Preface
by

Sis. Tauheedah S. Najee-Ullah El

Islam.

I rise giving All Perfect Praise to Allah, and Honors to His Prophet in these days, the Noble Prophet Drew Ali, and his forerunner, the Honorable Marcus Mosiah Garvey.

Allah indeed is the BEST of planners. The Bro. Rami Salaam El was introduced to me during a turbulent time professionally, I go about Allah's works and to who do likewise are well aware of the trials put on our path. Unsure of how to proceed, the Bro. Salaam El confirmed I was on the right path—he too, as it turned out, wanted to work on a compilation of literature standard to Moors on their quest to learn more of the M.S.T. of A. and its purpose.

We agreed that what should be readily available texts are proving too difficult for Moors to access, particularly those with no Temples or Study Groups in their area, as in Bro. Salaam's case. My added experience taught me that even when there are many bodies in ones areas, that is no guarantee it will not be difficult to access these vital books.

A final issue I've encountered too many times—the information contained in one Body's "version" differs from the many others in circulation. I learned this when I relocated to Los Angeles from Chicago and was able to make the comparison. Another examples of this is the use of "part and partial" versus "part and parcel." The former exists in law while the latter does not. One aim of this text is to eradicate these discrepancies.

As commanded by the Prophet, I got myself a good European education—in more than one discipline. Two of these are Education and History. I like to teach, will not do so unless using reliable sources. Based on the aforementioned reasons, I asked Allah guidance in leading me to original releases of the books the Moors so greatly desired. In His Grace and Mercy, He gave me just that: the contents of this text are reproductions of original printings and/ or reprinted from an original copy.

What's new may not be true; If it's old, you've probably got gold.

Peace & Love

Sis. Najee-Ullah El

Introduction

by G.S. Bro. Rami Abdullah Salaam El

With the help of Allah, His Universal Prophets Noble Drew Ali, Muhammad, Jesus, Confucius, Buddha, and assisted by Sis. Tauheedah S. Najee-Ullah El of Califa Media, We the People of the Moorish Divine & National Movement present to you Califa Uhuru: A Compilation of Literature from the Moorish Science Temple of America.

In this endeavor, We bring together the Holy Koran Circle 7, The Mysteries of the Silent Brotherhood of the East, Koran Questions for Moorish Americans—101s and 102s; The Divine Constitution, the Divine Warning By the Prophet (Noble Drew Ali) for the Nations, and the Hadith and Prophesies of Noble Drew Ali. In days past, one would have to search all over for these texts, at times having to piece them together. Now we've bound these Five into One . To make it plain (as a Wise Man once said), our aim is to make this Divine and National information accessible to the people as easily as possible. The time is now.

Thank You,
With Love
Rami Abdullah Salaam El

12. *The words of Buddha are recorded in the Indian sacred books. Attendeth them for they are part of the instructions of the Holy Breath.*
13. *The land of Egypt is the land of secret things.*
14. *The mysteries of the sages lie lock-bound in our Temples and Shrines.*
15. *The masters of all times and climes come here to learn. And when your sons have grown to manhood, they will finish all their studies in Egyptian schools.*
16. *But I have said enough. Tomorrow at the rising of the sun, we meet again.*

The Red Book, Chapter VII

Editor's Note

How to use this guide.

So that you may make most effective use of the instructions contained in this guide, I encourage the reader to have close at hand the following:

- A good standard dictionary of the English language, preferably one printed before 1965. The reason for this suggestion are two-fold: First, the book you hold is revised from a text originally published in 1928. Some of the word contained herein may no longer be in common use and/ or may have a different definition in modern dictionaries. Second, I suggest using a dictionary of this sort as many definitions—especially those pertaining to our people—were altered after the Civil Rights Movement in the United States. An example would be comparing the definitions of "American" in a pre-1965 dictionary versus one printed more recently.
    - Please note, there is no glossary contained in this guide to encourage use of the dictionary. Man—nor woman— knows not by being told.
- A Concordance of the Bible. As stated above, not all words are used correctly in these days and times. Additionally, words as used in the Bible should not be assumed to be the same used in common conversation.
- A Holy Quran of Mecca. The Prophet Noble Drew Ali did not release the Holy Koran of the Moorish Science Temple of America Circle Seven until between 1926 and 1928. The Moorish Holy Temple of Science, predecessor of the Moorish Science Temple of America, was founded in 1913 (Key 9). One must therefore ask themselves, what was the Prophet teaching from prior to the release of the Circle 7? The use of the Holy Quran of Mecca is further validated by its reference on our M.S.T. of A. Nationality Card: "*I do hereby declare that you are a Moslem under the divine Laws of the Holy Koran of Mecca...*"
- A bible of your choice.

As you read this guide you will notice spaces to the exterior of the pages. These are reserved for any notes you may wish to make. Scholarly works encourage the student to make notes next to the item being noted for quick future reference.

Willing you much success in your endeavor to improve yourself, and thereby, our Nation,

Peace & Love

Sis. Tauheedah S. Najee-Ullah El

I. Holy Koran of the Moorish Science Temple of America—Circle Seven

Divinely Prepared by the Noble Prophet Drew Ali

Source:

Noble Drew Ali, Prophet. *The Holy Koran of the Moorish Holy Temple of Science—Circle 7.* Prepared for publication by Sis. Tauheedah S. Najee-Ullah El. Redondo Beach, CA: Califa Media, 2014.

Know Thyself and Allah.

The Genealogy of "Jesus"
Life & Works of Jesus in India, Europe, and Africa, in the Land of Egypt.

Noble Drew Ali

The Prophet & Founder of Moorish Science Temple of America, To Redeem the People from Their Sinful Ways

Know Thyself
And Thy Father God Allah

The genealogy of Jesus with eighteen years of the events, life works and teachings in India, Europe and Africa. These events occurred before He was thirty years of age. These secret lessons are for all of those who love Jesus and desire to know about his life works and teachings.

Dear readers, do not falsely use these lessons. They are for good, peace and happiness for all those that love Jesus.

Dear mothers, teach these lessons to your little ones, that they may learn to love instead of hate.

Dear fathers, by these lessons you can set your house in order and your children will learn to love instead of hate.

The lessons of this pamphlet are not for sale, but for the sake of humanity, as I am a prophet and the servant is worthy of his hire, you can receive this pamphlet at expense. The reason these lessons have not been known is because the Moslems of India, Egypt and Palestine had these secrets and kept them back from the outside world, and when the time appointed by Allah they loosened the keys and freed the secrets, and for the first time in ages have these secrets been delivered in the hands of the Moslems of America. All authority and rights of publishing of this pamphlet of 1927.

By the Prophet

NOBLE DREW ALI

The industrious acts of the Moslems of the northwest and southwest Africa. These are the Moabites, Hamathites, Canaanites, who were driven out of the land of Canaan, by Joshua, and received permission from the Pharaohs of Egypt to settle in that portion of Egypt. In later years they formed themselves kingdoms. These kingdoms are called this day Morocco, Algiers, Tunis, Tripoli, etc.

CHAPTER I.

The Creation And Fall Of Man

"Time never was when man was not." If life of man at any time began, a time would come when it would end. "The thoughts of Allah cannot be circumscribed. No finite mind can comprehend things infinite. All finite things are subject unto change. All finite things will cease to be because there was a time when they were not." The bodies and the souls of men are finite things, and they will change, yea, from the finite point of view the time will come when they will be no more. "But man himself is not the body, nor the soul; he is a spirit and a part of Allah." Creative Fate gave to man, to spirit-man, a soul that he might function on the plane of soul; gave him a body of the flesh, that he might function on the plane of things made manifest. "Why did creative Fate give to spirit-man a soul that he might function on the plane of soul? Why did creative Fate give to soul a body of the flesh that he might function on the plane of things that are made manifest? Hear, mow, ye cherubim, ye seraphim, ye angels and ye men!

"Hear, now, oh protoplast, and earth, and plant and beast!

"Hear, now, ye creeping things of earth, ye fish that swim, ye birds that fly!

"Hear, now, ye winds that blow, ye thunders and ye lightnings of the sky!

"Hear, now, ye spirits of the fire, of water, earth, and air!

"Hear, now, oh everything that is, or was, or evermore will be, for wisdom speaks from out of the highest plane of spirit life:

"Man is a thought of Allah; all thoughts of Allah are infinite; they are not measured up by time, for things that are concerned with time, begin and end.

"The thoughts of Allah are the everlasting of the past unto the never ending days to come. And so is man, the spirit-man.

"But man like every other thought of Allah, was but a seed, a seed that held within itself the potencies of Allah, just as the seed of any plant of earth holds deep within itself the attributes of every part of that especial plant.

"So spirit-man, as seed of Allah held deep within himself the attributes of every part of Allah.

"Now, seed are perfect, yea, as perfect as the source from which they come; but they are not unfolded into life made manifest. The child is as perfect as the mother is. So man, the seed, must be deep planted in a soil that he might grow, unfold, as does the bud unfold to show the flower. The human seed that came forth from the heart of Allah was full ordained to be the Lord of plane of soul, and of the plane of things made manifest. So Allah, the husbandman of every thing that is, threw forth this human seed into the soil of soul; it grew apace, and man became a living soul; and he became the Lord of all the kingdom of the soul. Hark, now, let every creature hear, the plane of soul is but the ether of the spirit plane vibrating not so fast, and in the slower rhythm of this plane the essences of life are manifest; the perfumes and the odors, the true sensations and the all of love are manifest.

"And these soul attributes become a body beautiful. A multitude of lessons man must learn upon the plane of soul; and here he tarries many ages until his lessons are all learned. Upon the boundary of the plane of soul; there he must overcome, yea, overcome them every one. [The ether began to vibrate slower still and then the] essences took on a final garb; the perfumes and the odors and the true sensations and the all of love were clothed in flesh; and man was clothed in flesh. Perfected man must pass through all the ways of life, and so a carnal nature was full manifest, a nature that sprang forth from fleshly things. Without a foe a soldier never knows his strength, and thought must be developed by the exercise of strength. And so this carnal nature soon became a foe that man must fight, that he might be the strength of Allah made manifest. Let every living thing stand still and hear! Man is the Lord of all the plane of manifest, of protoplast, of mineral, of plant, of beast; but he gave up his birthrights, just to gratify his lower self. But man will regain his lost estate, his heritage; but he must do it in a conflict that cannot be told in words. Yet he must suffer trials and temptations manifold; but let him know that cherubim and seraphim that rule the stations of the sun and spirit of the mighty Allah who rule the solar stars are his protectors and his guide, and they will lead to victory. Man will be fully saved, redeemed, perfected by the things he suffers on the plane of flesh, and on the plane of soul. When man has conquered carnal things his garb of flesh will then have served its purpose well and it will fall; will be no more.

"Then he will stand untrammeled on the plane of soul where he must full complete his victories. Unnumbered foes will stand before man upon the plane of soul; these he must overcome, yea, overcome them every one. Thus hope will ever be his beacon light; there is no failure for the human soul, for Allah is leading on and victory is sure.

"Man cannot die; the spirit-man is one with Allah, and while Allah lives man cannot die. When man has conquered every foe upon the plane of soul the seed will have full opened out, will have unfolded in the Holy Breath. The garb of soul will then have served its purpose well, and man will need it never more, and it will pass and be no more and man will then attain unto the blessedness of perfectness and be at one with Allah."

CHAPTER II.

EDUCATION OF MARY AND ELIZABETH IN ZOAN, EGYPT

1. The son of Herod, Archelaus, reigned in Jerusalem. He was a selfish, cruel king; he put to death all those who did not honor him.

2. He called in council all the wisest men and asked [of] the infant claimant to his throne.

3. The council said that John and Jesus both were dead; then he was satisfied.

4. Now Joseph, Mary and their son were down in Egypt in Zoan, and John was with his mother in the Judean Hills.

5. Elihu and Salome sent messengers in haste to find Elizabeth and John. They found them, they brought them to Zoan.

6. Now Mary and Elizabeth were marveling much because of their deliverance.

7. Elihu said, "It is not strange; there are no happenings; law governs all events."

8. From olden times it was ordained that you should be with us and in this sacred school be taught.

9. Elihu and Salome took Mary and Elizabeth out to the sacred grove nearby where they were wont to teach.

10. Elihu said to Mary and Elizabeth, you may esteem yourself thrice blessed, for you are chosen mothers of long promised sons.

11. Who are ordained to lay a solid rock a sure foundation stone on which the temple of the perfect man shall rest—a temple that shall never be destroyed.

12. We measure time by cycle ages, and the gate to every age we deem a mile stone in the journey of the race.

13. An age had passed; the gate unto another age flies open at the touch of time. This is the preparation age of soul, the kingdom of Immanuel, of Allah in man.

14. And these, your sons, will be the first to tell the news, and teach the gospel of good will to men, and peace on earth.

15. A mighty work is theirs, for carnal men want not the light; they love the dark, and when the light shines in the dark they comprehend it not.

16. We call these sons Revealers of the Light, but they must have the light before they can receive the light.

17. And you must teach your sons, and set their souls on fire with love and holy zeal, and make them conscious of their missions to the sons of men.

18. Teach them that Allah and man are one, but that through carnal thoughts and words and deeds, man tore himself away from Allah, debased himself.

19. Teach that the Holy Breath would make them one again, restoring harmony and peace.

20. That naught can make them one but Love; that Allah so loved the world that He has clothed His son in flesh that man can comprehend.

21. The only Savior of the world is love; and Jesus, son of Mary, comes to manifest that love to men.

22. Now, love cannot manifest until its way has been prepared, and naught can rend the rock and bring down lofty hills and fill the valleys up, and thus prepare the way, but purity.

23. But purity in life men do not comprehend; and so, it, too, must come in flesh.

24. And you, Elizabeth, are blessed because yours is purity made flesh, and he shall pave the way for love.

25. This age will comprehend but little of the works of purity and love; but not a word is lost, for in the book of Allah's remembrance a registry is made of every thought and word and deed.

26. And when the world is ready to receive, lo, Allah will send a messenger to open the book and copy from its sacred pages all the messages of purity and love.

27. Then every man of earth will read the words of life in language of his native land, and men will see the light, walk in the light and be the light.

28. And man again will be at one with Allah."

CHAPTER III.

ELIHU'S LESSONS - THE UNITY OF LIFE

1. Again Elihu met his pupils in the sacred grove and said:

2. No man lives unto himself, for every living thing is bound by cords to every other living thing.

3. Blessed are the pure in heart; for they will love and not demand love in return.

4. They will not do to other men what they would not have other men do unto them.

5. There are two selves; the higher and the lower self.

6. The higher self is human spirit clothed with soul, made in the form of Allah.

7. The lower self, the carnal self, the body of desires, is a reflection of higher self, distorted by the murky ethers of the flesh.

8. The lower self is an illusion and will pass away; the higher self is Allah in man, and will not pass away.

9. The higher self is the embodiment of truth, the lower self is truth reversed and so is falsehood manifest.

10. The higher self is justice, mercy, love and right; the lower self is what the higher self is not.

11. The lower self breeds hatred, slander, lewdness, murders, theft, and everything that harms, the higher self is mother of the virtues and the harmonies of life.

12. The lower self is rich in promises, but poor in blessedness and peace; it offers pleasure, joy and satisfying gain; but gives unrest, misery and death.

13. It gives men apples that are lovely to the eye and pleasant to the smell; their cores are full of bitterness and gall.

14. If you would ask me what to study, I would say, yourselves; and when you well have studied them; and then would ask me what to study next, I would reply, yourselves.

15. He who knows well his lower self, knows the illusions of the world, knows of the things that pass away; and he knows his higher self, knows Allah; knows well the things that cannot pass away.

16. Thrice blessed is the man who has made purity and love his very own; he has been ransomed from the perils of the lower self and is himself his higher self.

17. Men seek salvation from an evil that they deem a living monster of the nether world; and they have gods that are but demons in disguise all powerful, yet full of jealousy and hate and lust;

18. Whose favors must be bought with costly sacrifice of fruits, and of the lives of birds, and animals, and human kind.

19. And yet these gods possess no ears to hear, no eyes to see, no heart to sympathize, no power to save.

20. This evil is a myth; these gods are made of air, clothed with shadows of a thought.

21. The only devil from which men must be redeemed is self, the lower self. If man would find his devil he must look within; his name is self.

22. If man would find his savior he must look within; and when the demon self has been dethroned the savior, love, will be exulted to the throne of power.

23. The David of the light is purity, who slays the strong Goliath of the dark, and seats the savior, love, upon the throne.

CHAPTER IV.

DEATH AND BURIAL OF ELIZABETH--MATHENO'S LESSONS --THE MINISTRY OF DEATH

1. When John was twelve years old his mother died, and neighbors laid her body in a tomb among her kindred in the Hebron burying ground, and near the Zacharias tomb.

2. And John was deeply grieved; he wept. Matheno said, it is not well to weep because of death.

3. Death is no enemy of man; it is a friend who, when the work of life is done, just cuts the cord that binds the human boat to earth, that it may sail on smoother seas.

4. No language can describe a mother's worth, and yours was tried and true. But she was not called hence until her tasks were done.

5. The calls of death are always for the best, for we are solving problems there as well as here; and one is sure to find himself where he can solve his problems best.

6. It is but selfishness that makes one wish to call again to earth departed souls.

7. Then let your mother rest in peace. Just let her noble life be strengthened and inspiration unto you.

8. A crisis in your life has come, and you must have a clear conception of the work that you are called to do.

9. The sages of the ages call you harbinger. The Prophets look to you and say, "He is Elijah come again."

10. Your mission here is that of harbinger; for you will go before the Messiah's face to pave his way, and make the people ready to receive their king.

11. This readiness is purity of heart; none but the pure in heart can recognize the king.

12. To teach men to be pure in heart, you must yourself be pure in heart and word and deed.

13. In infancy the vow for you was made and you became a Nazarite. The razor shall not touch your face nor head, and you shall taste not wine nor fiery drinks.

14. Men need a pattern for their lives; they love to follow, not to lead.

15. The man who stands upon the corners of the paths and points the way, but does not go, is just a pointer; and a block of wood can do the same.

16. The teacher treads the way; on every span of ground he leaves his foot-prints, clearly cut, which all can see and be assured that he, their master went that way.

17. Men comprehend the inner life by what they see and do. They come to Allah through ceremonies and forms.

18. And so when you would make men know that sins are washed away by purity in life, a rite symbolic may be introduced.

19. In water wash the bodies of the people who would turn away from sin and strive for purity in life.

20. This rite of cleansing is a preparation rite and they who thus are cleansed comprise the temple of purity.

21. And you shall say, You men of Israel, hear; reform and wash; become the sons of purity, and you shall be forgiven.

22. This rite of cleansing and this temple are but symbolic of the cleansing of the soul, which does not come from outward show, but is the temple within.

23. Now, you may never point the way and tell the multitudes to do what you have never done; but you must go before and show the way.

24. You are to teach that men must wash; so you must lead the way, your body must be washed, symbolic of the cleansing of the soul."

25. John said, Why need I wait? May I not go at once and wash?

26. Matheno said: "Tis well", and then they went down to the Jordan ford, and east of Jericho, just where the host of Israel crossed when first they entered Canaan, they tarried for a time.

27. Matheno taught the harbinger, and he explained to him the inner meaning of the cleansing rite and how to wash himself and how to wash the multitude.

28. And in the river Jordan, John was washed; then they returned unto the wilderness.

29. Now in Engedi's hills Matheno's work was done and he and John went down to Egypt. They rested not until they reached the Temple of Sakara in the valley of the Nile.

30. For many years, Matheno was a master in this temple of the Brotherhood, and when he told about the life of John and of his mission to the sons of men, the hierophant with joy received the harbinger and he was called the Brother Nazarite.

31. For eighteen years John lived and wrought within these temple gates; and here he conquered self, became a master mind and learned the duties of the harbinger.

Chapter V

After the feast--The Homeward Journey--The Missing Jesus--The Search For Him. His Parents Find Him In the Temple--He Goes With Them To Nazareth--Symbolic Meaning of Carpenter's Tools.

1. The great Feast of the Pasch was ended and the Nazarenes were journeying toward their homes.

2. And they were in Samaria, and Mary said: "Where is my son?" No one had seen the boy.

3. And Joseph sought among their kindred who were on their way to Galilee; but they had seen him not.

4. Then Joseph, Mary, and a son of Zebedee returned and sought through all Jerusalem, but they could find him not.

5. And Mary asked the guards had they seen Jesus, a little boy about twelve years old.

6. The guards replied: "Yes, he is in the temple now disputing with the doctors of the law."

7. And they went in, and found him as the guards had said.

8. And Mary said: "Why, Jesus, why do you treat your parents thus? Lo, we have sought two days for you. We feared that some great harm had overtaken you."

9. And Jesus said, "Do you not know that I must be about my Father's work?"

10. But He went round and pressed the hand of every doctor of the law and said: "I trust that we meet again."

11. And then he went forth with his parents on their way to Nazareth; and when they reached their home He wrought with Joseph as a carpenter.

12. One day as He was bringing forth the tools for work he said:

13. "These tools remind me of the ones we handle in the workshop of the mind where things were made of thought and where we build up character.

14. We use the square to measure all our lines, to straighten out the crooked places of the way, and make the corners of our conduct square.

15. We use the compass to draw circles around our passions and desires to keep them in the bounds of righteousness.

16. We use the axe to cut away the knotty, useless and ungainly parts and make the character symmetrical.

17. We use the hammer to drive home the truth, and pound it in until it is a part of every part.

18. We use the plane to smooth the rough, uneven surfaces of joint, and block, and board that go to build the temple for the truth.

19. The chisel, line, the plummet and the saw all have their uses in the workshop of the mind.

20. And then this ladder with its trinity of steps, faith, hope and love; on it we climb up to the dome of purity in life.

21. And on the twelve step ladder, we ascend until we reach the pinnacle of that which life is spent to build the Temple of Perfected Man."

Chapter VI
Life and Works of Jesus in India Among the Moslems

1. A royal prince of India, Ravanna in the South, was at the Jewish Feast.
2. Ravanna was a man of wealth, and he was just, and with a band of Brahmic priests sought wisdom in the west.
3. When Jesus stood among the Jewish priests and read and spoke, Ravanna heard and was amazed.
4. And when he asked who Jesus was, from whence He came and what He was, Chief Hillel said:
5. "We call this child the Day Star from on high, for He has come to bring to men a light, the light of life; to lighten up the way of men and to redeem His people of Israel."
6. And Hillel told Ravanna all about the child; about the prophecies concerning Him; about the wonders of the night when He was born; about the visit of the Magian priests.
7. About the way in which He was protected from the wrath of evil men; about His flight to Egyptland, and how He then was serving with His father as a carpenter in Nazareth.
8. Ravanna was entranced, and asked to know the way to Nazareth, that he might go and honor such a one as son of Allah.
9. And with his gorgeous train he journeyed and came to Nazareth of Galilee.
10. He found the object of his search engaged in building dwellings for the sons of men.
11. And when he first saw Jesus He was climbing up a twelve step ladder, and He carried in His hands a compass, square and axe.
12. Ravanna said: "All hail, most favored son of Heaven!"
13. And at the inn Ravanna made a feast for all the people of the town; and Jesus and His parents were honored guests.
14. For certain days Ravanna was a guest in Joseph's home on Marmion Way; he sought to learn the secret of the wisdom of the son; but it was all to great for him.
15. And then he asked that he might be the patron of the child, might take Him to the east, where He could learn the wisdom of the Brahms.

16. And Jesus longed to go, that He might learn; and after many days His parents gave consent.

17. Then, with proud heart, Ravanna with his train, began the journey towards the rising sun; and after many days they crossed the sand, and reached the province of Orissa, and the palace of the prince.

18. The Brahmic priests were glad to welcome home the prince; with favor they received the Jewish boy.

19. And Jesus was accepted as a pupil in the Temple Jagannath; and here He learned the Vedas and the Manic law.

20. The Brahmic Masters wondered at the clear conceptions of the Child, and often were amazed when He explained to them the meaning of the law.

CHAPTER VII

The Friendship of Jesus and Lamaas--Jesus Explains to Lamaas the Meaning of Truth

1. Among the priests of Jagannath was one who loved the Jewish boy. Lamaas Bramas was the name by which the priest was known.
2. One day as Jesus and Lamaas walked alone in Plaza Jagannath, Lamaas said: "My Jewish master, what is truth?"
3. And Jesus said: "Truth is the only thing that changes not.
4. In all the world there are two things; The one is truth; the other is falsehood, and falsehood that which seems to be.
5. Now truth is aught and has no cause, and yet it is the cause of everything.
6. Falsehood is naught, and yet it is the manifest of right.
7. Whatever has been made will be unmade; that which begins must end.
8. All things that can be seen by human eyes are manifests of aught, are naught, and so must pass away.
9. The things we see are but reflexes just appearing, while the ethers vibrate so and so, and when conditions change they disappear.
10. The Holy Breath is truth; is that which was, and is, and evermore shall be; it cannot change nor pass away."
11. Lamaas said: "You answer well, now what is man?"
12. And Jesus said, "Man is the truth and falsehood strangely mixed.
13. Man is the Breath made flesh; so truth and falsehood are conjoined in him; and they strive, and naught goes down and man as truth abides."
14. Again Lamaas asked: "What do you say of power?"
15. And Jesus said: "It is a manifest; is the result of force; it is but naught; it is illusion, nothing more. Force changes not, but power changes as the ethers change.
16. "Force is the will of Allah and is omnipotent, and power is that will in manifest, directed by the Breath."

17. "There is power in the winds, a power in the waves, a power in the lightning's stroke, a power in the human arm, a power in the eye."

18. "The ethers cause these powers to be, and thought of Elohim, of angel, man, or other thinking things, directs the force; when it has done its work the power is no more."

19. Again Lamaas asked: "Of understanding, what have you to say?"

20. And Jesus said: "It is the rock on which man builds himself; it is the Gnosis of the aught and of the naught, of falsehood and of truth."

21. "It is the knowledge of the lower self; the sensing of the powers of man himself."

22. Again Lamaas asked: "Of wisdom what have you to say?"

23. And Jesus said: "It is the consciousness that man is aught; that Allah and man are one;

24. That naught is naught; that power is but illusion; that heaven and earth and hell are not above, around, below, but in; which in the light of aught becomes the naught, and Allah is all."

25. Lamaas asked: "Pray, what is faith?"

26. And Jesus said: "Faith is the surety of the omnipotence of Allah and man; the certainty that man will reach the deific life.

27. Salvation is a ladder reaching from the heart of man to heart of Allah.

28. It has three steps; Belief is first, and this is what man thinks, perhaps, is truth.

29. And faith is next, and this is what man knows is truth.

30. Fruition is the last, and this is man himself, the truth.

31. Belief is lost in faith; and in fruition is lost; and man is saved when he has reached deific life; when he and Allah are one."

Chapter VIII

Jesus Reveals to the People of Their Sinful Ways

1. In all the cities of Orissa Jesus taught. At Katak, by the river side, He taught, and thousands of the people followed him.

2 One day a car of Jagannath was hauled along by scores of frenzied men, and Jesus said:

3. "Behold, a form without a spirit passes by; a body with no soul; a temple with no altar fires.

4. This car of Krishna is an empty thing, for Krishna is not there.

5. This car is but an idol of a people drunk on wine of carnal things.

6. Allah lives not in the noise of tongues; there is no way to Him from any idol shrine.

7. Allah's meeting place with man is in the heart, and in a still small voice he speaks; and he who hears is still."

8. And all the people said: "Teach us to know the Holy One who speaks within the heart, Allah of the still small voice."

9. And Jesus said, "The Holy Breath cannot be seen with mortal eyes; nor can men see the spirits of the Holy One.

10. But in their image man was made, and he who looks into the face of man, looks at the image of the Allah who speaks within.

11. And when man honors man, he honors Allah, and what man does for man he does for Allah.

12. And you must bear in mind that when man harms in thought or word or deed another man, he does a wrong to Allah.

13. If you would serve the Allah who speaks within the heart, just serve your near of kin, and those that are no kin, the stranger at your gates, the foe who seeks to do you harm.

14. Assist the poor, and help the weak; do harm to none, and covet not what is not yours.

15. Then, with your tongue the Holy One will speak; and he will smile behind your tears, will light your countenance with joy, and fill your hearts with peace."

16. And then the people asked: "To whom shall we bring gifts? Where shall we offer sacrifice?"

17. And Jesus said: "Our Father--Allah asks not for needless waste of plant, of grain, of dove, of lamb.

18. That which you burn on any shrine you throw away. No blessings can attend the one who takes the food from hungry mouths to be destroyed by fire.

19. When you would offer sacrifice unto Allah, just take your gift of grain, or meat, and lay it on the table of the poor.

20. From it an incense will arise to heaven, which will return to you with blessedness.

21. Tear down your idols; they can hear you not; turn all your sacrificial altars into fuel for the flames.

22. Make human hearts your altars, and burn your sacrifices with the fire of love."

23. And all the people were entranced, and would have worshiped Jesus as a God; but Jesus said:

24. "I am your brother man just come to show the way to Allah; you shall not worship man; praise Allah the Holy One."

CHAPTER IX

Jesus attends a feast in Behar and Here He Taught Human Equality.

1. The fame of Jesus as a teacher spread through all the land, and people came from near and far to hear His words of truth.
2. At Behar, on the sacred river of the Brahms, he taught for many days.
3. And Ach, a wealthy man of Behar, made a feast in honor of his guest, and he invited every one to come.
4. And many came; among them thieves, extortioners, and courtesans. And Jesus sat with them and taught; but they who followed him were much aggrieved, because He sat with thieves and courtesans.
5. And they upbraided Him; they said: "Rabboni, master of the wise, this day will be an evil day for you.
6. The news will spread that you consort with courtesans and men will shun you as they shun an asp."
7. And Jesus answered them and said: "A master never screens himself for sake of reputation or of fame.
8. These are but worthless baubles of the day; they arise and sink, like empty bottles on a stream; they are illusions and will pass away;
9. They are the indices to what the thoughtless think; they are the noise that people make; and shallow men judge merit by the noise.
10. Allah and all master men judge men by what they are and not by what they seem to be; not by their reputation and their fame.
11. These courtesans and thieves are children of my Father Allah; their soul are just as precious in His sight as yours, or of the Brahmic priests.
12. And they are working out the same life sums that you have solved, you men who look at them with scorn.
13. And some of them have solved much harder sums than you have solved, you men who look at them with scorn.
14. Yes, they are sinners, and confess their guilt while you are guilty, but are shrewd enough to have a polished coat to cover up your guilt.

15. Suppose you men who scorn the courtesans, these drunkards and these thieves, who know that you are pure in heart and life, that you are better far than they, stand forth that men may know just who you are.

16. The sin lies in the wish, in the desire, not in the act.

17. You covet other people's wealth; you look at charming forms, and deep within your hearts you lust for them.

18. Deceit you practice every day, and wish for gold, for honor and for fame, just for your selfish selves.

19. The man who covets is a thief, and she who lusts is courtesan. You who are none of these speak out."

20. Nobody spoke; the accusers held their peace.

21. And Jesus said: "The proof this day is all against those who have accused.

22. The pure in heart do not accuse. The vile in heart who want to cover up their guilt with holy smoke of piety are ever loathing drunkard, thief and courtesans.

23. This loathing and this scorn is mockery, for if the tinseled coat of reputation could be torn away, the loud professor would be found to revel in his lust, deceit and many forms of secret sin.

24. The man who spends his time in pulling other people's weeds can have no time to pull his own, and all the choicest flowers of life will soon be choked and die, and nothing will remain but darnel, thistles and burs."

25. And Jesus spoke a parable; He said: "Behold, a farmer had great fields of ripened grain, and when he looked he saw that blades of many stalks of wheat were bent and broken down.

26. And when he sent his reapers forth he said 'We will not save the stalks of wheat that have the broken blades.

27. Go forth and cut and burn the stalks with broken blades.'

28. And after many days he went to measure up his grain, but not a kernel could he find.

29. And then he called the harvesters and said to them: 'Where is my grain?'

30. They answered him and said: 'We did according to your word; we gathered up and burned the stalks with broken blades, and not a stalk was left to carry to the barn.'

31. And Jesus said: "If Allah saves only those who have no broken blades, who have been perfected in His sight, who will be saved?"

32. And the accusers hung their heads in shame; and Jesus went His way.

CHAPTER X

Jesus Spake on the Unity of Allah and Man to the Hindus

1. Benares is the sacred city of the Brahms, and in Benares Jesus taught; Udraka was His host.

2. Udraka made a feast in honour of his guests, and many high born Hindu priests and scribes were there.

3. And Jesus said to them, with much delight "I speak to you concerning life--the brotherhood of life.

4. The universal Allah is one, yet He is more than one; all things are one.

5. By the sweet breath of Allah all life is bound in one; so if you touch a fiber of a living thing you send a thrill from the center to the outer bounds of life.

6. And when you crush beneath your foot the meanest worm, you shake the throne of Allah, and cause the sword of life to tremble in its sheath.

7. The bird sings out its song for men, and men vibrate in unison to help it sing.

8. The ant constructs her home, the bee its sheltering comb, the spider weaves her web and flowers breath to them a spirit in their sweet perfume that gives them strength to toil.

9. Now, men and birds and beasts and creeping things are deities, made flesh; and how dare men kill anything?

10. It is cruelty that makes the world awry, when men have learned that when they harm a living thing, they harm themselves, they surely will not kill, nor cause a thing that Allah has made to suffer pain."

11. A lawyer said: "I pray to Jesus, tell who is this Allah you speak about; where are His priests, His temples and His shrines?"

12. And Jesus said: "The Allah I speak about is everywhere; He cannot be compassed with walls, nor hedged about with bounds of any kind.

13. All people worship Allah, the One; but all the people see Him not alike.

14. This universal Allah is wisdom, will and love.

15. All men see not the Triune Allah. One sees Him as Allah of might; another as Allah of thought; another as Allah of love.

16. A man's ideal is his God, and so, as man unfolds, his God unfolds. Man's God today, tomorrow is not God.

17. The nations of the earth see Allah from different points of view, and so He does not seem the same to every one.

18. Man names the part of Allah he sees, and this to him is all of Allah; and every nation sees a part of Allah, and every nation has a name for Allah.

19. You Brahmans call Him Parabrahm; in Egypt he is Thoth; and Zeus is His name in Greece, Jehovah is His Hebrew name; but everywhere He is the causeless cause, the rootless root from which all things have grown.

20. When men are afraid of Allah and take Him for a foe, they dress up other men in fancy garbs and call them priests.

21. And charge them to restrain the wrath of Allah by prayers and when they fail to win His favour by their prayers, to buy Him off with sacrifice of animals or birds.

22. When man sees Allah as one with him, as Father Allah, he needs no middle man, no priest to intercede.

23. He goes straight up to Him and says, 'My Father God, Allah!' and then he lays his hand in Allah's own hand, and all is well.

24. And this is Allah. You are, each one, a priest, just for yourself; and sacrifice of blood Allah does not want.

25. Just give your life in sacrificial service to all of life, and Allah is pleased."

26. When Jesus had thus said He stood aside; the people were amazed, but strove among themselves.

27. Some said: "He is inspired by Holy Brahm" and others said: "He is insane"; and others said: "He is obsessed; he speaks as devils speak."

28. But Jesus tarried not. Among the guests was one, a tiller of the soil, a generous soul, a seeker after truth, who loved the words that Jesus spoke, and Jesus went with him and in his home abode.

Chapter XI

Jesus and Barata--Together They Read the Sacred Books.

1. Among the Buddhist priests was one who saw a lofty wisdom in the words that Jesus spoke. It was Barata Arabo.

2. Together Jesus and Barata read the Jewish Psalms and prophets; read the Vedas, the Avesta and the wisdom of Gautama.

3. And as they read and talked about the possibilities of man, Barata said:

4. "Man is the marvel of the universe. He is part of everything, for he has been a living thing on every plane of life.

5. Time was when man was not; and then he was bit of formless substance in the molds of time; and then a protoplast.

6. By universal law, all things tend upward to a state of perfectness. The protoplast evolved, becoming worm, then reptile, bird and beast, and then at last it reached the form of man.

7. Now, man himself is mind, and mind is here to gain perfection by experience; and mind is often manifest in fleshy form, and in the form best suited to its growth. So mind may manifest as worm, or bird, or beast, or man.

8. The time will come when everything of life will be evolved unto the state of perfect man.

9. And after man is man in perfectness, he will evolve to higher forms of life."

10. And Jesus said: "Barata Arabo, who taught you this, that mind which is the man, may manifest in flesh of beast, or bird, or creeping thing?"

11. Barata said: "From times which man remembers not our priests have told us so, and so we know."

12. And Jesus said: "Enlightened Arabo, are you a master mind and do not know that man knows naught by being told?

13. Man may believe what others say, but thus he never knows. If man would know, he must, himself be what he knows.

14. Do you remember, Arabo, when you were ape, or bird, or worm?

15. Now, if you have no better proving of your plea than that the priests have told you so, you do not know; you simply guess.

16. Regard not, then, what any man has said; let us forget the flesh, and go with mind into the land of fleshless things; mind never does forget.

17. And backward through the ages master minds can trace themselves; and thus they know.

18. Time never was when man was not.

19. That which begins will have an end. If man was not, the time will come when he will not exist.

20. From Allah's own Record Book we read: The Triune Allah breathed forth, and stood seven spirits before His face. The Hebrews call these seven Spirits, Elohim.

21. And these are they who, in their boundless power, created everything that is, or was.

22. These Spirits of the Triune Allah moved on the face of boundless space and seven others were and every other had its form of life.

23. These forms of life were but the thought of Allah, clothed in the substance of their ether planes.

24. Men call these ether planes the planes of protoplast, of earth, of plant, of beast, of man, of angel and of cherubim.

25. These planes with all their teeming thoughts of Allah, are never seen by eyes of man in flesh; they are composed of substance far too fine for fleshy eyes to see, and still they constitute the soul of things.

26. And with the eyes of soul all creatures see these ether planes, and all forms of life.

27. Because all forms of life on every plane are thoughts of Allah, all creatures think, and every creature is possessed of will, and, in its measure, has the power to choose.

28. And in their native planes all creatures are supplied with nourishment from the ethers of their planes.

29. And so it was with every living thing until the will became a sluggish will, and then the ethers of the protoplast, the earth, the plant, the beast, the man, began to vibrate very slow.

30. The ethers all became more dense, and all the creatures of these planes were clothed with coarser garbs of flesh, which men can see; and thus this coarser manifest, which men call physical, appeared.

31. And this is what is called the fall of man; but man fell not alone for protoplast, and earth, and plant and beast were all included in the fall.

32. The angels and the cherubim fell not; their wills were ever strong, and so they held the ethers of their planes in harmony with Allah.

33. Now, when the ether reached the rate of atmosphere, and all the creatures of these planes must get their food from atmosphere, the conflict came; and that which the finite man called, survival of the best, became the law.

34. The stronger ate the bodies of the weaker manifests; and here is where the carnal law of evolution had its rise.

35. And now man, in his utter shamelessness, strikes down and eats the beasts, the beast consumes the plant, the plant thrives on the earth, the earth absorbs the protoplast.

36. In yonder kingdom of the soul this carnal evolution is not known, and the great work of master minds is to restore the heritage of man, to bring him back to his estate that he has lost, when he again will live upon the ethers of his native plane.

37. The thoughts of Allah change not; the manifests of life on every plane unfold into perfection of their kind; and as the thought of Allah can never die, there is no death to any being of the seven ethers of the seven Spirits of the Triune Allah.

38. And so an earth is never plant; a beast, or bird, or creeping thing is never man, and man is not, and cannot be, a beast, or bird, or creeping thing.

39. The time will come when all these seven manifests will be absorbed, and man and beast and plant and earth and protoplast will be redeemed."

40. Barata was amazed; the wisdom of the Jewish sage was a revelation unto him.

41. Now, Vidyapati, wisest of the Indian sages, chief of temple Kapavistu, heard Barata speak to Jesus of the origin of man, and heard the answer of the Hebrew prophet, and he said:

42. "You priests of Kapavistu, hear me speak; we stand to-day upon a crest of time. Six times ago a master soul was born who gave a glorious light to man, and now a master sage stands here in the temple Kapavistu.

43. The Hebrew prophet is the rising star of wisdom, deified. He brings to us a knowledge of the secrets things of Allah; and all the world will hear his words, will heed his words, and glorify his name.

44. You priests of temple Kapavistu, stay; be still and listen when he speaks; he is the living Oracle of Allah."

45. And all the priests gave thanks, and praised the Buddha of enlightenment.

Fig. No. 1

CHAPTER XII

Jesus Teaches the Common People at a Spring--Tells Them How to Obtain Eternal Happiness.

1. In silent meditation Jesus sat beside a flowing spring. It was a holy day, and many people of the servant caste were near the place.

2. And Jesus saw the hard drawn lines of toil on every brow, in every hand. There was no look of joy in any face. Not one of all the group could think of anything but toil.

3. And Jesus spoke to one and said: "Why are you all so sad? Have you no happiness in life?"

4. The man replied: "We scarcely know the meaning of that word. We toil to live, and hope for nothing else but toil, and bless the day when we can cease our toil and lay down and rest in Buddha's city of the dead."

5. And Jesus' heart was stirred with pity and with love for these poor toilers, and he said:

6. "Toil should not make a person sad; men should be happiest when they toil. When hope and love are back of toil then all of life is filled with joy and peace and this is heaven. Do you not know that such a heaven is for you?"

7. The man replied: "Of heaven we have heard; but then it is so far away, and we must live so many lives before we can reach that place!"

8. And Jesus said: "My brother, man, your thoughts are wrong; your heaven is not far away, and it is not a place of metes and bounds, is not a country to be reached; it is a state of mind!

9. Allah never made a heaven for man; He never made a hell; we are creators and we make our own.

10. Now cease to seek for heaven in the sky; just open up the windows of the hearts, and, like a flood of light, a heaven will come and bring a boundless joy; then toil will be no cruel task."

11. The people were amazed, and gathered close to hear this strange young master speak,

12. Imploring him to tell them more about the Father-God, Allah, about the heaven that men can make on earth; about the boundless joy.

13. And Jesus spoke a parable; he said: "A certain man possessed a field; the soil was hard and poor.

14. By constant toil he scarcely could provide enough of food to keep his family from want.

15. One day a miner who could see beneath the soil, in passing on his way, saw this poor man and his unfruitful field.

16. He called the weary toiler and he said: 'My brother, know you not that just below the surface of your barren field rich treasures lie concealed?

17. You plough and sow and reap in a scanty way, and day by day you tread upon a mine of gold and precious stones.

18. This wealth lies not upon the surface of the ground; but if you will dig away the rocky soil, and delve down deep into the earth, you need no longer till the soil for naught.'

19. The man believed. 'The miner surely knows,' 'And I will find the treasures hidden in my field.'

20. And then he dug away the rocky soil, and deep down in the earth he found a mine of gold."

21. And Jesus said: "The sons of men are toiling hard on desert plains, and burning sands and rocky soils, are doing what there fathers did, not dreaming they can do aught else.

22. Behold a master comes, and tells them of a hidden wealth; that underneath the rocky soil of carnal things are treasures that no man can count.

23. That in the heart the richest gems abound; that he who wills may open the door and find them all."

24. And then the people said: "Make known to us the way that we may find the wealth that lies within the heart."

25. And Jesus opened up the way; the toilers saw another side of life, and toil became a joy.

Chapter XIII

Life and Works of Jesus In Egypt Among the Gentiles

1. Jesus with Elihu and Salome in Egypt. Tells the story of his journeys. Elihu and Salome praise Allah. Jesus goes to the temple in Heliopolis and is received as a pupil.

2. And Jesus came to Egyptland and all was well. He tarried not upon the coast; He went at once to Zoan, home of Elihu and Salome, who five and twenty years before had taught His mother in their sacred school.

3. And there was joy when met these three. When last the son of Mary saw these sacred groves he was a babe;

4. And now a man grown strong by buffeting of every kind; a teacher who had stirred the multitudes in many lands.

5. And Jesus told the aged teachers all about His life; about his journeyings in foreign lands; about the meetings with the masters and about His kind receptions by the multitudes.

6. Elihu and Salome heard His story with delight; they lifted up their eyes to heaven and said: "Our Father-God Allah, let now Thy servants go in peace, for we have seen the glory of Allah.

7. And we have talked with Him, the messenger of love, and of the covenant of peace on earth, good will to men.

8. Through Him shall all the nations of the earth be blessed; through Him, Immanuel."

9. And Jesus stayed in Zoan many days; and then went forth unto the city of the sun, that men call Heliopolis, and sought admission to the temple of the sacred brotherhood.

10. The council of the brotherhood convened, and Jesus stood before the hierophant; He answered all the questions that were asked with clearness and with power.

11. The hierophant exclaimed: "Rabboni of the rabbinate, why come you here? Your wisdom is the wisdom of the gods; why seek for wisdom in the halls of men?"

12. And Jesus said: "In every way of earth-life I would walk; in every hall of learning I would sit; the heights that any man has gained, these I would gain.

13. What any man has suffered I would meet, that I may know the griefs, the disappointments and the sore temptations of my brother man; that I may know just how to succor those in need.

14. I pray you brothers, let me go into your dismal crypts; and I would pass the hardest of your tests."

15. The master said: "Take then the vow of secret brotherhood." And Jesus took the vow of secret brotherhood.

16. Again the master spoke; he said: "The greatest heights are gained by those who reach the greatest depths; and you shall reach the greatest depths."

17. The guide then led the way and in the fountain Jesus bathed; and when He had been clothed in proper garb He stood again before the hierophant.

CHAPTER XIV

John, the Harbinger, Returns to Hebron, Lives as a Hermit In the Wilds, Visits Jerusalem and Speaks to the People.

1. It came to pass when John, the son of Zacharias and Elizabeth, had finished all his studies in the Egyptian schools he returned to Hebron, where he abode for certain days.

2. And then he sought the wilderness and made his home in David's cave, where many years before he was instructed by the Egyptian sage.

3. Some people called him Hermit of Engedi; and others said, "He is the wild man of the hills."

4. He clothed himself with skins of beasts; his food was carobs, honey, nuts and fruits.

5. When John was thirty years of age he went into Jerusalem, and in the market place he sat in silence seven days.

6. The common people and the priests, the scribes and Pharisees came out in multitudes to see the silent hermit of the hills; but none were bold enough to ask him who he was.

7. But when his silent past was done he stood forth in the midst of all and said:

8."Behold the King has come; the prophets told of Him; the wise men long have looked for Him.

9. Prepare, O Israel, prepare to meet your King."

10. And that was all he said, and then he disappeared, and no one knew where he had gone.

11. And there was great unrest through all Jerusalem. The rulers heard the story of the hermit of the hills.

12. And they sent couriers forth to talk with him that they might know about the coming King; but they could find him not.

13. And after certain days he came again into the market place, and all the city came to hear him speak. He said:

14. "Be not disturbed, you rulers of the state; the coming King is no antagonist; he seeks no place on any earthly throne."

[He comes the Prince of Peace, the king of righteousness and love; his kingdom is with in the soul.]

15. "The eyes of men shall see it not and none can enter but the pure in heart."

16. "Prepare, O Israel, prepare to meet your King."

17. Again, the hermit disappeared; the people strove to follow him, but he had drawn a veil about his form and men could see him not.

18. Jewish feast day came; Jerusalem was filled with Jews and proselytes from every part of Palestine, and John stood in the temple court and said:

19. "Prepare, O Israel, prepare to meet your King."

20. "So, you have lived in sin; the poor cry in your streets, and you regard them not.

21. Your neighbors, who are they? You have defrauded friends and foes alike.

22. You worship Allah with voice and lip; your hearts are far away, and set on gold.

23. Your priests have bound upon the people burdens far to great to bear; they live in ease upon the hard earned wages of the poor.

24. Your lawyers, doctors, scribes are useless cumberers of the ground; they are but tumors on the body of the state.

25. They toil not, neither do they spin, yet they consume the profits of your marts of trade.

26. Your rulers are adulterers, extortioners and thieves, regarding not the rights of any man.

27. And robbers ply their calling in the sacred hills; the holy temple you have sold to thieves; their dens are in the sacred places set apart for prayer.

28. Hear! hear! You people of Jerusalem! Reform: turn from your evil ways or Allah will turn from you, and heathen from afar will come, and what is left of all your honor and your fame will pass in one short hour."

29. "Prepare, Jerusalem, prepare to meet your King."

30. He said no more; he left the court and no one saw him go.

31. The priests, the doctors and the scribes were all in rage. They sought for John, intent to do him harm. They found him not.

[The common people stood in his defense; they said: "The hermit speaks the truth.

And then the priests, the doctors and the scribes were sore afraid; they said no more; they hid themselves away.]

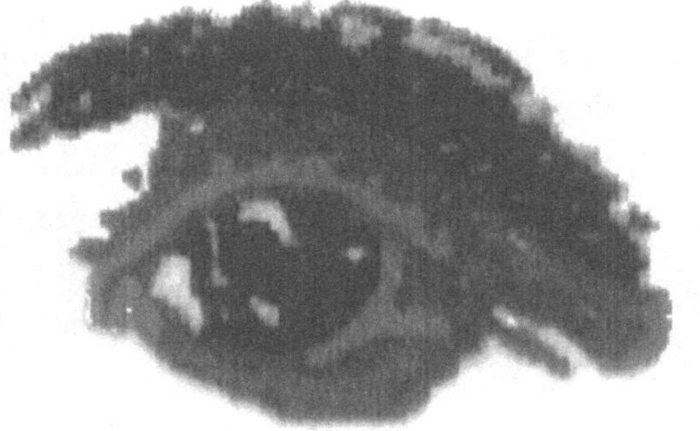

CHAPTER XV

Jesus Goes to the Wilderness For Self-examination, Where He Remains Forty Days--Is Subjected to Three Temptations. He Overcomes--Returns to the Camps of John and Begins Teaching.

1. The harbinger had paved the way; the Logos had been introduced to men as love made manifest, and he must now begin his divine ministry.

2. And he went forth into the wilderness to be alone with Allah, that He might look into His inner heart, and note its strength and worthiness.

3. And with Himself He talked; He said: "My lower self is strong; by many ties I am bound down to carnal life.

4. Have I the strength to overcome and give my life a willing sacrifice for men?

5. When I shall stand before the face of men, and they demand a proof of my Messiahship, what will I say?"

6. And then the tempter came and said: "If you be son of Allah, command these stones to turn to bread."

7. And Jesus said: "Who is it that demands a test? It is no sign that one is Son of Allah because he does a miracle; the devils can do mighty things.

8. Did not the Gentile magicians do great things before the Pharaoh?

9. My words and deeds in all the walks of life shall be the proof of my Messiahship."

10. And then the tempter said: "If you will go into Jerusalem, and from the temple pinnacle cast down yourself to earth, the people will believe that you are the Messiah sent from Allah.

11. This you can surely do; for did not David say: 'He gives His angels charge concerning you, and with their will they uphold lest you should fall?"

12. And Jesus said: "I may not tempt the Lord, my God, Allah."

13. And then the tempter said: "Look forth upon the world; behold its honors and its fame! Behold its pleasures and its wealth!

14. If you will give your life for these they shall be yours."

15. But Jesus said: "Away from me all tempting thoughts. My heart is fixed. I spurn this carnal self with all its vain ambition and its pride."

16. For forty days did Jesus wrestle with His carnal self; His higher self Prevailed. He then was hungry, but his friends had found Him and they ministered to Him.

17. Then Jesus left the wilderness and in the consciousness of Holy breath, he came unto the camps of John and taught.

CHAPTER XVI

Pilate's Final Effort to Release Jesus Fails--He Washes His Hands In Feigned Innocence--Delivers Jesus to the Jews For Execution--The Jewish Soldiers Drive Him to Calvary.

1. A superstitious people are the Jews. They have a faith that they have borrowed from the idol worshipers of other lands, that at the end of every year,

2. They may heap all their sins upon the head of some man set apart to bear their sins.

3. The man becomes a scapegoat for the multitudes; and they believe that when they drive him forth into the wilds, or into foreign lands, they are released from sins.

4. So every spring before the feast they chose a prisoner from the prisons of the land, and by a form their own, they fain would make him bear their sins away.

5. Among the Jewish prisoners in Jerusalem were three who were the leaders of a vile, seditious band, who had engaged in thefts and murders and rapine, and had been sentenced to be crucified.

6. Barabbas and Jezia was among the men who were to die; but Barabbas was rich and he had bought off priests the boon to be scapegoat for the people at the coming feast, and he was anxiously in waiting for his hour to come.

7. Now, Pilate thought to turn this superstition to account to save the Lord Jesus, and so he went again before the Jews and said:

8. "You men of Israel, according to my custom I will release to you today a prisoner who shall bear you sins away.

9. This man you drive into the wilds or into foreign lands, and you have asked me to release Barabbas, who has been proven guilty of the murder of a score of men.

10. Now, hear me men. Let Jesus be released and let Barabbas pay his debt upon the cross; then you can send this Jesus to the wilds and hear no more of Him."

11. At what the ruler said the people were enraged, and they began to plot to tear the Roman palace down and drive in exile Pilate, and his household and his guards.

12. When Pilate was assured that civil war would follow if he heeded not the wishes of the mob, he took a bowl of water and in the presence of the multitude he washed his hands and said:

13. "This man whom you accuse is Son of the Most High Allah, and I proclaim my innocence.

14. If you would shed His blood, His blood is on your hands and not on mine."

15. And then the Jews exclaimed: "And let His blood be on our hands and on our children's hands."

16. And Pilate trembled like a leaf, in fear. Barabbas he released, and as the Lord stood forth before the mob, the ruler said: "Behold your King! And would you put to death your King?"

17. The Jews replied, "He is no King; we have no King but great Tiberius."

18. Now, Pilate would not give consent that Roman soldiers should imbue their hands in blood of innocence and so the chief priests and the Pharisees took counsel what to do with Jesus.

19. Caiaphas has said: "We cannot crucify this man; he must be stoned to death and nothing more."

20. And then the rabble said: "Make haste! let Him be stoned." And then they led Him forth toward the hill beyond the city's gates, where criminals were put to death.

21. The rabble could not wait until they reached the place of skulls. As soon as they had passed the city's gates, they rushed upon Him, smote Him with their hands, they spit upon Him, stoned Him and He fell upon the ground.

22. And one, a man of Allah, stood forth and said: "Isaiah said, He shall be bruised for our transgressions and by His stripes we shall be healed."

23. As Jesus laid all bruised and mangled on the ground a High Priest called out, "Stay, stay you men! Behold the guards of Herod come and they will crucify this man."

24. And there beside the city's gate they found Barabbas' cross, and then the frenzied mob cried out, "Let him be crucified."

25. Caiaphas and the other ruling Jews came forth and gave consent.

26. And then they lifted Jesus from the ground, and at the point of swords they drove Him on.

27. A man named Simon, from Cyrene, a friend of Jesus, was near the scene, and since the bruised and wounded Jesus could not bear His cross, they laid it on the shoulders of this man and made him bear it on to Calvary.

CHAPTER XVII

Jesus Appears, Fully Materialized, Before Apollo and the Silent Brotherhood In Greece--Appears to Claudia and Juliet On the Tiber Near Rome--Appears to the Priest In the Egyptian Temple at Heliopolis.

1. Apollo, with the Silent Brotherhood of Greece, was sitting in a Delphian grove. The Oracle had spoken loud and long.

2. The priests were in the sanctuary and as they looked the Oracle became a blaze of light; it seemed to be on fire, and all consumed.

3. The priests were filled with fear. They said: "A great disaster is to come; our gods are mad; they have destroyed our Oracle.

4. But when the flames had spent themselves, a man stood on the Oracle's pedestal and said:

5. "Allah speaks to man, not by an oracle of wood and gold, but by the voice of man."

6. "The gods have spoken to the Greeks, and kindred tongues, through images made by man, but Allah the One, now speaks to man through Jesus the only Son, who was, and is and evermore will be.

7. This Oracle shall fail; the living Oracle of Allah, the One, will not fail."

8. Apollo knew the man who spoke; he knew it was the Nazarene who once had taught the wise men in the Acropolis and had rebuked the idol worshipers upon the Athens' beach.

9. And in a moment Jesus stood before Apollo and the Silent Brotherhood and said:

10. "Behold, for I have risen from the dead with gifts for men. I bring to you the title of your vast estate.

11. All power in heaven and earth is mine; to you I give all power in heaven and earth.

12. Go forth and teach the nations of the earth the Gospel of the resurrection of the dead and of eternal life through Jesus, the love of Allah made manifest to men."

13. And then he clasped Apollo's hand and said: "My human flesh was changed to higher form by love divine and I can manifest in flesh or in the higher planes of life at will.

14. What I can do all men can do. Go teach the Gospel of the Omnipotence of man."

15. Then Jesus disappeared; but Greece and Crete and all the nations heard.

16. Claudas and Juliet, his wife, lived on the Palatine in Rome and they were servants of Tiberius; but they had been in Galilee.

17. Had walked with Jesus by the sea, had heard His words and seen His power; and they believed that He was Jesus made manifest.

18. Now Claudas and his wife were on the Tiber in a little boat; a storm swept from the sea, the boat was wrecked and Claudas and his wife were sinking down to death.

19. And Jesus came and took them by the hands and said: "Claudas and Juliet, arise and walk with me upon the waves."

20. And they arose and walked with him upon the waves.

21. A thousand people saw three walk on the waves, and saw them reach the land, and they were all amazed.

22. And Jesus said: "You men of Rome, I am the resurrection and the life. They that are dead shall live, and many that shall live will never die.

23. By mouth of gods and demi-gods Allah spoke unto your fathers long ago; but now He speaks to you through perfect man."

24. "He sent His son, Jesus, in human flesh to save the world, and as I lifted from the watery grave and saved these servants of Tiberius.

20. So Jesus will lift the sons and daughters of the human race, yea every one of them, from darkness and from graves of carnal things, to light and everlasting life.

26. I am the manifest of love raised from the dead; Behold my hands, my feet, my side which carnal men have pierced.

27. Claudas and Juliet whom I have saved from death, are my ambassadors to Rome.

28. And they will point the way and preach the gospel of the Holy Breath and the resurrection of the dead."

29. And that was all he said, but Rome and all of Italy heard.

30. The priests of Heliopolis were in their temple met to celebrate the resurrection of their brother Nazarite; they knew that he had risen from the dead.

31. The Nazarite appeared and stood upon a sacred pedestal on which no man had ever stood.

32. This was an honor that had been reserved for him who first would demonstrate the resurrection of the dead.

33. And Jesus was the first of all the human race to demonstrate the resurrection of the dead.

34. When Jesus stood upon the sacred pedestal the masters stood and said, "All hail!" The great bells of the temple rang and all the temple was ablaze with light.

35. And Jesus said: "All honor to the masters of this Temple of the Sun.

36. In flesh of man there is the essence of the resurrection of the dead. This essence quickened by the Holy Breath, will raise the substance of the Body to a higher tone,

37. And make it like the substance of the bodies of the planes above, which human eyes cannot behold.

38. There is a holy ministry in death. The essence of the body cannot be quickened by the Holy Breath until the fixed is solved; the body must disintegrate, and this is death.

39. And then upon these pliant substances Allah breathes, just as he breathed upon the chaos of the deep when worlds were formed.

40. And life springs forth from death; the carnal form is changed to form divine.

41. The will of man makes possible the action of the Holy Breath. When will of man and will of Allah are one, the resurrection is a fact.

42. In this we have the chemistry of mortal life, the ministry of death, the mystery of deific life.

43. My human life was wholly given to bring my will to tune with the deific will; when this was done my earth-tasks all were done.

44. And you, my brother, know full well the foes I had to meet; you know about my victories in Gethsemane; my trials in the courts of men; my death upon the cross.

45. You know that all my life was one great drama for the sons of men; a pattern for the sons of men. I lived to show the possibilities of man.

46. What I have done all men can do, and what I am all men shall be."

47. The masters looked; the form upon the sacred pedestal had gone, but every temple priest, and every living creature said: "Praise Allah."

CHAPTER XVIII

The Resurrection of Jesus--Pilate Places the Roman Seal Upon the Stone Door Of the Tomb--At Mid-night a Company Of the Silent Brothers March About the Tomb--The Soldiers Are Alarmed--Jesus Preaches To the Spirits In Prison--Early Sunday Morning He Rises From the Tomb--The Soldiers Are Bribed By the Priests To Say That the Disciples Had Stolen the Body.

The tomb in which they laid the body of the Lord was in a garden, rich with flowers, the garden of Saloam, and Joseph's home was near.

2. Before the watch began Caiaphas sent a company of priests out to the garden of Saloam that they might be assured that Jesus' body was within the tomb.

3. They rolled away the stone; they saw the body there, and then they placed the stone again before the door.

4. And Pilate sent his scribe who placed upon the stone the seal of Rome, in such a way that he who moved the stone would break the seal.

5. To break this Roman seal meant death to him who broke the seal.

6. The Jewish soldiers all were sworn to faithfulness; and then the watch began.

7. At midnight all was well, but suddenly the tomb became a blaze of light, and down the garden walk a troupe of white clad soldiers marched in single file.

8. They came up to the tomb and marched and countermarched before the door.

9. The Jewish soldiers were alert; they thought His friends had come to steal the body of the Nazarene. The captain of the guard cried out to charge.

10. They charged; but not a white clad soldier fell. They did not even stop; they marched and countermarched among the frightened men.

11. They stood upon the Roman seal; they did not speak ; they unsheathed not their swords; it was the Silent Brotherhood.

12. The Jewish soldiers fled in fear; they fell upon the ground.

13. They stood apart until the white clad soldiers marched away, and then the light about the tomb grew dim.

14. Then, they returned; the stone was in its place; the seal was not disturbed, and they resumed their watch.

15. Now, Jesus did not sleep within the tomb. The body is the manifest of soul; but soul is without its manifest.

16. And in the realm of souls, unmanifest, the Lord went forth and taught.

17. He opened up the prison doors and set the prisoners free.

18. He broke the chains of captive souls, and led the captives to the light.

19. He sat in council with the patriarchs and prophets of the olden times.

20. The masters of all times and climes He met, and in the great assemblies he stood forth and told the story of His life on earth, and of his death in sacrifice for man,

21. And of his promises to clothe himself again in garb of flesh and walk with his disciples, just to prove the possibilities of man.

22. To give to them the key of life, of death and of the resurrection of the dead.

23. In council all the masters sat and talked about the revelations of the coming age,

24. When she, the Holy Breath, shall fill the earth and air with holy breath, and open up the way of man to perfectness and endless life.

25. The garden of Saloam was silent on the Sabbath day. The Jewish soldiers watched and no one else approached the tomb; but on the following night the scene was changed.

26. At midnight every Jewish soldier heard a voice which said. "Adon Mashich Cumi," which meant: "Lord Jesus arise.

27. And they supposed again the friends of Jesus were alert, were coming up to take the body of their Lord away.

28. The soldiers were alert with swords unsheathed and drawn, and then they heard the words again.

29. It seemed as though the voice was everywhere, and yet they saw no man.

30. The soldiers blanched with fear, and still to flee meant death for cowardice, and so they stood and watched.

31. Again, and this was just before the sun arose, the heavens blazed with light: a distant thunder seemed to herald forth a coming storm.

32. And then the earth began to quake and in the rays of light they saw a form descend from heaven. They said: "Behold, an angel comes."

33. And then they heard again: "Adon Mashich Cumi."

34. And then the white-robed form tramped on the Roman seal, and then he tore it into shreds, he took the mighty stone in his hand as though it were a pebble from the brook, and cast it to the side.

35. And Jesus opened up His eyes and said, "All hail the rising sun; the coming of the day of righteousness!"

36. And then He folded up His burial gown, His head bands and His coverings and laid them all aside.

37. He arose, and for a moment stood beside the white-robed form.

38. The weaker soldiers fell to the ground, and hid their faces in their hands; the stronger stood and watched.

39. They saw the body of the Nazarene transmute. They saw it change from mortal to immortal form, and then it disappeared.

40. The soldiers heard a voice from somewhere; yea, from everywhere, it said:

41. "Peace, peace on earth; good will to men."

42. They looked, the tomb was empty and the Lord had risen as He said.

43. The soldiers hastened to Jerusalem, and to the priests, and said:

44. "Behold the Nazarene has risen as He said; the tomb is empty and the body of the man is gone; we know not where it is." And then they told about the wonders of the night.

45. Caiaphas called a council of the Jews, he said: "The news must not go forth that Jesus has arisen from the dead.

46. For if it does, all men will say: "He is the son of Allah, and all our testimonials will be proven false."

47. And then they called the hundred soldiers in and said to them:

48. "You know not where the body of the Nazarene is resting now, so if you will go forth and say that His disciples came and stole the body while you slept,

49. Each one of you shall have a silver piece, and we will make it right with Pilate for breaking of the Roman seal."

50. The soldiers did as they were paid to do.

CHAPTER XIX

Jesus Appears, Fully Materialised, To the Eastern Sages In the Palace Of Prince Ravanna In India--To the Magian Priests In Persia. --The Three Wise Men Speak In Praise Of the Personality Of the Nazarene.

1. Ravanna, prince of India, gave a feast. His palace in Orissa was the place where men of thought from all the farther East were wont to meet.

2. Ravanna was the prince with whom the child Jesus went to India with when twelve years old.

3. The feast was made in honor of the wise men of the East.

4. Among the guests were Mengste, Vidyapati and Lamaas.

5. The wise men sat about the table talking of the needs of India and the world.

6. The door unto the banquet hall was in the East; a vacant chair was at the table to the East.

7. And as the wise men talked a stranger entered, unannounced, and raising up his hands in benediction said, "All hail!"

8. A halo rested on his head, and light, unlike the light of sun, filled all the room.

[9.The wise men rose and bowed their heads and said, "All hail!"]

10. And Jesus sat down in the vacant chair; and then the wise men knew it was the Jewish Prophet who had come.

11. And Jesus said: "Behold, for I am risen from the dead. Look at my hands, my feet, my side.

12. The Roman soldiers pierced my hands and feet with nails; and then one pierced my heart.

13. They put me in a tomb, and then I wrestled with the conqueror of men. I conquered death, I stamped upon him and arose.

14. Brought immortality to light and painted on the walls of time a rainbow for the sons of men; and what I did all men shall do.

15. This gospel of the resurrection of the dead is not confined to Jew and Greek; it is the heritage of every man of every time and clime; and I am here a demonstrator of the power of man."

16. Then He arose and pressed the hand of every man and of the royal host, and said:

17. "Behold, I am not myth made of the fleeting winds, for I am flesh and bone and brawn; but I can cross the borderland at will."

18. And then they talked together there a long, long time. Then Jesus said:

19. "I go my way, but you shall go to all the world and teach the gospel of the omnipotence of men, the power of truth, the resurrection of the dead.

20. He who believes this gospel of the son of man shall never die; the dead shall live again."

21. Then Jesus disappeared, but He had sown the seed. The words of life were spoken in Orissa, and all of India heard.

22. The Magian priests were in the silence in Persepolis, and Kaspar, and the Magian masters, who were first to greet the child of promise in the shepherd's home in Bethlehem, were with the priests.

23. And Jesus came and sat with them; a crown of light was on His head.

24. And when the silence ended Kaspar said: "A master from the Royal Council of the Silent Brotherhood is here; let us give praise."

25. And all the priests and masters stood and said: "All hail! What message from the Royal Council do you bring?"

26. And Jesus said: "My brothers of the Silent Brotherhood, peace, peace on earth, good will to men!

27. The problem of the age has been solved; a son of man risen from the dead; has shown that human flesh can be transformed into flesh divine.

28. Before the eyes of men this flesh in which I come to you was changed with speed of light from human flesh. And so I am the message that I bring to you.

29. To you I come, the first of all the race to be transmuted to the image of Allah.

30. What I have done, all men will do; and what I am, all men shall be."

31. But Jesus said no more. In one short breath He told the story of His mission to the sons of men, and then He disappeared.

32. The Magi said: "Some time ago we read this promise, now fulfilled, upon the dial plate of Heaven.

33. And then we saw this man who has just demonstrated unto us the power of man to raise from carnal flesh and blood to flesh of Allah, a babe in Bethlehem.

34. And after many years He came and sat with us in these same groves;

35. He told the story of His human life, of trials, sore temptations, buffeting and woes.

36. He pressed along the thorny way of life 'till He had risen and overthrown the strongest foes of Allah and man; and He is now the only master of the human race whose flesh has been transmuted into flesh divine.

37. He is the God-man of to-day; but everyone of earth shall overcome and be like Him, a Son of Allah.

Epilogue for Chapters II-XIX

These events occurred before He was thirty years of age, and the events after He had risen from the dead. He appeared back to India, Europe and Africa in the land of Egypt, and made himself known unto the world. These events are the eighteen years which are absent in your "Holy Bible." The events of John the Baptist. John taught by the Egyptian sage. The meaning of baptism and how to baptize himself. And after he was baptized, he was taken at the age of twelve years into Africa, the land of Egypt, and there he remained in the Egyptian schools eighteen years. And there he learned his duty as "fore-runner of Jesus."

CHAPTER XX

HOLY INSTRUCTION AND WARNINGS FOR ALL YOUNG MEN

1. Beware, young man, beware of all the allurements of wantonness, and let not the harlot tempt thee to excess in her delights.

2. The madness of desire shall defeat its own pursuits; from the blindness of its rage, thou shalt rush upon destruction.

3. Therefore give not up thy heart to her sweet enticements, neither suffer thy soul to be enslaved by her enchanting delusions

4. The fountain of health which must supply the stream of pleasure, shall quickly be dried up, and every spring of joy shall be exhausted.

5. In the prime of thy life old age shall overtake thee; the sun shall decline in the morning of thy days.

6. But when virtue and modesty enlighten her charms, the luster of a beautiful woman is brighter than the stars of Heaven and the influence of her power it is in vain to resist.

7. The whiteness of her bosom transcendeth the lily; her smile is more delicious than a garden of roses.

8. The innocence of her eyes is like that of the turtle; simplicity and truth dwell in her heart.

9. The kisses of her mouth are sweeter than honey; the perfumes of Arabia breathe from her lips.

10. Shut not thy bosom to the tenderness of love; the purity of its flame shall ennoble thy heart, and soften it to receive the fairest impressions.

CHAPTER XXI

MARRIAGE INSTRUCTIONS FOR MAN AND WIFE FROM THE NOBLE PROPHET

1. Give ear, fair daughter of love, to the instructions of prudence and let the precepts of truth sink deep in thy heart; so shall the charms of thy mind add luster to the elegance of thy form; and thy beauty, like the rose it resembleth, shall retain its sweetness when its bloom is withered.

2. In the spring of thy youth, in the morning of thy days, when the eyes of men gaze on thee with delight, and nature whispereth in thine ear the meaning of their looks; ah, hear with caution their seducing words; guard well thy heart, nor listen to their soft persuasions.

3. Remember thou art made man's reasonable companion, not the slave of his passion; the end of thy being is not merely to gratify his loose desire; but to assist him in the toils of life, to soothe his heart with thy tenderness and recompense his care with soft endearments.

4. Who is she that winneth the heart of man, that subdueth him to love, and reigneth in his breast?

5. Lo! Yonder she walketh in maiden sweetness, with innocence in her mind, and modesty on her cheek.

6. Her hand seeketh employment, her foot delighteth not in gadding abroad.

7. She is clothed with neatness, she is fed with temperance; humility and meekness are as a crown of glory circling her head.

8. On her tongue dwelleth music, the sweetness of honey floweth from her lips. Decency is in all her words, in her answers are mildness and truth.

9. Submission and obedience are the lessons of her life, and peace and happiness are her reward.

10. Before her steps walketh prudence, and virtue attendeth at her right hand.

11. Her eye speaketh softness and love, but discretion with a sceptre sitteth on her brow.

12. The tongue of the licentious is dumb in her presence; the awe of her virtue keepeth him silent.

13. When scandal is busy, and the fame of her neighbors is tossed from tongue to tongue; if charity and good nature open not her mouth, the finger of silence resteth on her lip.

14. Her breast is the mansion of goodness, and therefore she suspecteth no evil of others.

15. Happy were the man that should make her his wife; happy the child that should call her mother.

16. She presideth in the house, and there is peace; she commandeth with judgment, and is obeyed.

17. She ariseth in the morning, she considers her affairs, and appointeth to every one their proper business.

18. The care of her family is her whole delight; to that alone she applieth her study; and elegance with frugality is seen in her mansion.

19. The prudence of her management is an honor to her husband, he heareth her praise with a secret delight.

20. She informeth the minds of her children with wisdom; she fashioneth their manners from the examples of her own goodness.

21. The words of her mouth is the law of their youth; the motion of her eye commandeth their obedience.

22. She speaketh, and the servants fly; she pointeth, and the thing is done; for the law of love is in their hearts, and her kindness addeth wings to their feet.

23. In prosperity she is not puffed up; in adversity she healeth the wounds of fortune with patience.

24. The troubles of her husband are alleviated by her councils and sweetened by her endearments; he putteth his heart in her bosom, and receiveth comfort.

25. Happy is the man that has made her his wife; happy the child that call her mother.

CHAPTER XXII

DUTY OF A HUSBAND

1. Take unto thyself a wife and obey the ordinance of Allah; take unto thyself a wife, and become a faithful member of society.

2. But examine with care, and fix not suddenly. On thy present choice depends thy future happiness.

3. If much of her time is destroyed in dress and adornment; if she is enamored with her own beauty, and delighted with her own praise; if she laugheth much, and talketh loud; if her foot abideth not in her father's house, and her eyes with boldness rove on the faces of men; though her beauty were as the sun in the firmament of heaven, turn thy face from her charms, turn thy feet from her paths, and suffer not thy soul to be ensnared by the allurements of imagination.

4. But when thou findest sensibility of heart, joined with softness of manners; and accomplished mind, with a form agreeable to thy fancy; take her home to thy house; she is worthy to be thy friend, thy companion in life, the wife of thy bosom.

5. O cherish her as a blessing sent to thee from Heaven. Let the kindness of thy behavior endear thee to her heart.

6. She is the mistress of thy house; treat her therefore with respect, that thy servants may obey her.

7. Oppose not her inclination without cause; she is the partner of thy cares, make her also the companion of thy pleasures.

8. Reprove her faults with gentleness, exact not her obedience with rigor.

9. Trust thy secrets in her breast; her counsels are sincere, thou shalt not be deceived.

10. Be faithful to her bed; for she is mother of thy children.

11. When pain and sickness assault her, let thy tenderness soothe her affliction; a look from thee of pity and love shall alleviate her grief, or instigate her pain and be of more avail than ten physicians.

12. Consider the tenderness of her sex, the delicacy of her frame; and be not severe to her weakness, but remember thine own imperfections.

CHAPTER XXIII

HOLY INSTRUCTIONS FOR THY CHILDREN

1. Consider, thou art a parent, the importance of thy trust; the being thou hast produced, it is thy duty to support.

2. Upon thee also it dependeth whether the child of thy bosom be a blessing or a curse to thyself; an useful or a worthless member to the community.

3. Prepare him early with instruction, and season his mind with the maxims of truth.

4. Watch the bent of his inclinations, set him right in his youth and let no evil habit gain strength with his years.

5. So shall he rise like a cedar on the mountains; his head shall be seen above the trees of the forest.

6. A wicked son is a reproach to his father; but he that doth right is an honor to his grey hairs.

7. The soil is thine own, let it not want cultivation; the seed which thou soweth, that also shall thou reap.

8. Teach him obedience, and he shall bless thee; teach him modesty, and he shall not be ashamed.

9. Teach him gratitude, and he shall receive benefits; teach him charity, and he shall gain love.

10. Teach him temperance, and he shall have health; teach him prudence, and fortune shall attend him.

11. Teach him justice, and he shall be honored by the world; teach him sincerity, and his own heart shall not reproach him.

12. Teach him diligence, and his wealth shall increase; teach him benevolence, and his mind shall be exalted.

13. Teach him science, and his life shall be useful; teach him religion, and his death shall be happy.

CHAPTER XXIV

THE OBEDIENCE OF CHILDREN TOWARDS THEIR FATHER

1. From the secrets of Allah let man learn wisdom, and apply to himself the instruction they give.

2. Go to the desert, my son; observe the young stork of the wilderness; let him speak to thy heart; he beareth on his wings his aged sire; he lodgeth him in safety, and supplieth him with food.

3. The piety of a child is sweeter than the incense of Persia offering to the sun; yea, more delicious than odors wafted from a field of Arabian spices of the western gales.

4. Be grateful to thy father, for he gave thee life and to thy mother, for she sustained thee.

5. Hear the words of his mouth, for they are spoken for thy good; give ear to his admonition, for it proceedeth from love.

6. He hath watched for thy welfare, he hath toiled for thy ease; do honor therefore to his age, and let not his grey hairs be treated with irreverence.

7. Forget not thy helpless infancy, nor the forwardness of thy youth, and indulge the infirmities of thy aged parents; assist and support them in the decline of life.

8. So shall their hoary heads go down to the grave in peace; and thine own children, in reverence of thy example, shall repay thy piety with filial love.

CHAPTER XXV
A HOLY COVENANT OF THE ASIATIC NATION

1. Ye are the children of one father, provided for by his care; and the breast of one mother hath given you suck.
2. Let the bonds of affection, therefore, unite thee with thy brothers, that peace and happiness may dwell in thy father's house.
3. And when ye separate in the world, remember the relation that bindeth you to love and unity; and prefer not a stranger before thy own blood.
4. If thy brother is in adversity, assist him; if thy sister is in trouble, forsake her not.
5. So shall the fortunes of thy father contribute to the support of his whole race; and his care be continued to you all, in your love to each other.

CHAPTER XXVI

HOLY INSTRUCTIONS OF UNITY

1. The gifts of the understanding are the treasures of Allah; and He appointed to every one his portion, in what measure seemeth good unto Himself.

2. Hath He endowed thee with wisdom? Hath He enlightened thy mind with the knowledge of truth? Communicate it to the ignorant, for their instruction; communicate it to the wise, for thine own improvement.

3. True wisdom is less presuming than folly. The wise man doubteth often, and changeth his mind; the fool is obstinate, and doubteth not; he knoweth all things, but his own ignorance.

4. The pride of emptiness is an abomination; and to talk much, is the foolishness of folly; nevertheless, it is the part of wisdom to hear with patience their impertinence, and to pity their absurdity.

5. Yet be not puffed up in thine own conceit, neither boast of superior understanding; the clearest human knowledge is but blindness and folly.

6. The wise man feeleth his imperfections, and is humbled; he laboreth in vain for his own approbation but the fool peepeth in the shadow stream of his own mind, and is pleased with the pebbles which he seeth at the bottom; he bringeth them up and showeth them as pearls and with the applause of his brethren delighteth himself.

7. He boasteth of attainments in things that are of no worth; but where it is a shame to be ignorant, there he hath no understanding.

8. Even in the path of wisdom, he toileth after folly; and shame and disappointment are the reward of his labor.

9. But the wise man cultivates his mind with knowledge; the improvement of the arts is his delight, and their utility to the public crowneth with honor.

10. Nevertheless, the attainment of virtue he accounteth as the highest learning; and the science of happiness is the study of his life.

CHAPTER XXVII

THE HOLY UNITY OF THE RICH AND THE POOR

1. The man to whom Allah hath given riches, and blessed with a mind to employ them alright, is peculiarly favored and highly distinguished.

2. He looketh on his wealth with pleasure, because it affordeth him the means to do good.

3. He protecteth the poor that are injured; he suffereth not the mighty to oppress the weak.

4. He seeketh out objects of compassion; he inquireth into their wants; he relieveth them with judgments and without ostentation.

5. He assisteth and rewardeth merit; he encourage ingenuity and liberally promoteth every useful design.

6. He carieth his own great works; his country is enriched, and the labor is employed; he formeth new schemes, and the arts receive improvement.

7. He considers the superfluities of his table, as belonging to the poor of his neighborhood; and he defraudeth them not.

8. The benevolence of his mind is not checked by his fortune; he rejoiceth therefore in riches, and his joy is blameless.

9. But woe. unto him that heapeth up wealth in abundance, and rejoiceth alone in the possession thereof; that grindeth the face of the poor, and considereth not the sweat of their brows!

10. He driveth on oppression, without feeling; the ruin of his brother disturbeth him not.

11. The tears of the orphan he drinketh as milk; the cries of the widow are music to his ears.

12. His heart hardened with the love of wealth; no grief or distress can make impression upon it.

13. But the curse of iniquity pursueth him; he liveth in continual fear; the anxiety of his mind and the rapacious desires of his own soul take vengeance upon him for the calamities he has brought upon others.

14. Oh! What are the miseries of poverty in comparison with the gnawings of this man's heart!

15. Let the poor man comfort himself, yes, rejoice; for he hath many reasons.

16. He sitteth down to his morsel in peace; his table is not crowded with flatterers and devourers.

17. He is not embarrassed with a train of dependents, nor teased with the clamors of solicitations.

18. Debarred from the dainties of the rich, he escapeth also their diseases.

19. The bread that he eateth is not so sweet to his taste? The water he drinketh is not so pleasant to his thirst? Yea, far more delicious water than the richest draughts of the luxurious.

20. His labor preserveth his health, and procureth him a repose, to which the downy bed of sloth is a stranger.

21. He limiteth his desires with humility, and the calm of contentment is sweeter to his soul than all the acquirements of wealth and grandeur.

22. Let not the rich, therefore, presume on his riches; nor the poor in his poverty yield to despondence; for the providence of Allah dispenseth happiness to them both.

CHAPTER XXVIII

HOLY INSTRUCTIONS FROM THE PROPHET

MASTER AND SERVANT

1. Repine not, 0 man, at the state of servitude; it is the appointment of Allah, and hath many advantages; it removeth thee from cares and solicitudes in life.

2. The honor of a servant is his fidelity; his highest virtues are submission and obedience.

3. Be patient, therefore, under the reproofs of thy master; and when he rebuketh thee, answer not again. The silence of thy resignation shall not be forgotten.

4. Be studious of his interests, be diligent in his affairs, and faithful to the trust which he reposeth in thee.

5. Thy time and thy labor belong unto him. Defraud him not thereof, for he payeth thee for them.

6. And thou who art a master, be just to thy servant if thou expecteth from him fidelity; and reasonable in thy commands if thou expecteth ready obedience.

7. The spirit of a man is in him; severity and rigour may create fear, but can never command love.

8. Mix kindness with reproof, and reason with authority; so shall thy admonitions take place in his heart, and his duty shall be-come his pleasure.

9. He shall serve thee faithfully from the motive of gratitude; he shall obey thee cheerfully from the principle of love; and fail thou not, in return, to give his diligence and fidelity their proper reward.

CHAPTER XXIX

MAGISTRATE AND SUBJECT

1. 0 thou, the favorite of Heaven, whom the sons of men, thy equals, have agreed to raise to sovereign power and set as a ruler over themselves; consider the ends and importance of their trust, fax more than the dignity and height of thy station.

2. Thou art clothed in purple, and seated on a throne; the crown of majesty investeth thy temples, the sceptre of power is placed in thy hand; but not for thyself were these ensigns given; not meant for thine own, but the good of thy kingdom.

3. The glory of a king is the welfare of his people; his power and dominion rest on the hearts of his subjects.

4. The mind of a great prince is exalted with the grandeur of his situation; he evolveth high things, and searcheth for business worthy of his power.

5. He calleth together the wise men of his kingdom; he consulteth among them with freedom, and heareth the opinions of them all.

6. He looketh among his people with discernment; he discovereth the abilities of men, and employeth them according to their merits.

7. His magistrates are just, his ministers are wise, and the favorite of his bosom deceiveth him not.

8. He smileth on the arts, and they flourish; the sciences improve beneath the culture of his hand.

9. With the learned and ingenious he delighteth himself; he kindleth in their breasts emulation; and the glory of his kingdom is exalted by their labors.

10. The spirit of the merchant who extendeth his commerce, the skill of the farmer who enricheth his lands, the ingenuity of the artists, the improvements of the scholar; all these he honoreth with his favor, or rewardeth with his bounty.

11. He planteth new colonies, he buildeth strong ships, he openeth rivers for convenience, he formeth harbors for safety, his people abound in riches, and the strength of his kingdom increaseth.

12. He frameth his statutes with equity and wisdom; his subjects enjoy the fruits of their labor in security; and their happiness consists of the observance of the law.

13. He foundeth his judgments on the principle of mercy; but in the punishment of offenders, he is strict and impartial.

14. His ears are open to the complaints of his subjects; he restraineth the hands of their oppressors, and he delivereth them from their tyranny.

15. His people, therefore, look up to him as a father, with reverence and love; they consider him as the guardian of all they enjoy.

16. Their affection unto him begetteth in his breast a love of the public; the security of their happiness is the object of his care.

17. No murmurs against him arise in their hearts; the machinations of his enemies endanger not the state.

18. His subjects are faithful, and firm in his cause; they stand in his defense, as a wall of brass; the army of a tyrant flieth before them, as chaff before the wind.

19. Security and peace bless the dwelling of his people; and glory and strength encircle his throne forever.

CHAPTER XXX

HOLY INSTRUCTION FROM THE PROPHET

THE SOCIAL DUTIES

1. When thou considereth thy wants, when thou beholdeth thy imperfections, acknowledge his goodness, 0 son of humanity, who honored thee with humanity, endowed thee with speech, and placed thee in society to receive and confer reciprocal helps and mutual obligations, protection from injuries, thy enjoyments of the comforts and the pleasures of life; all these thou oweth to the assistance of others, and couldst not enjoy but in the bands of society.

2. It is thy duty, therefore, to be a friend to mankind, as it is thy interest that man should be friendly to thee.

3. As the rose breatheth sweetness from its own nature, so the heart of a benevolent man produceth good works.

4. He enjoyeth the ease and tranquility of his own breast, and rejoiceth in the happiness and prosperity of his neighbor

5. He openeth not his ear unto slander; the faults and the failings of men give a pain to his heart.

6. His desire is to do good, and he researcheth out the occasions thereof; in removing the oppression of another, he relieveth himself.

7. From the largeness of his mind, he comprehendeth in his wishes the happiness of all men; and from the generosity of his heart, he endeavoreth to promote it.

CHAPTER XXXI

HOLY INSTRUCTIONS FROM THE PROPHET

JUSTICE

1. The peace of society dependeth on justice; the happiness of individuals, on the safe enjoyment of all their possessions.

2. Keep the desires of thy heart, therefore, within the bounds of moderation; let the hand of justice lead them aright.

3. Cast not an evil eye on the goods of thy neighbor; let whatever is his property be sacred from thy touch.

4. Let no temptation allure thee, nor any provocation excite thee to lift up thy hand to the hazard of his life.

5. Defame him not in his character; bear no false witness against him.

6. Corrupt not his servant to cheat or forsake him; and the wife of his bosom, 0 tempt not to sin.

7. It will be a grief to his heart, which thou canst not relieve; an injury to his life, which no reparation can atone.

8. In thy dealings with men, be impartial and just; and do unto them as thou wouldst they should do unto thee.

9. Be faithful to thy trust, and deceive not the man who relieth upon thee; be assured, it is less evil in the sight of Allah to steal than to betray.

10. Oppress not the poor, and defraud not of his hire the laboring man.

11. When thou selleth for gain, hear the whispering of conscience, and be satisfied with moderation; nor from the ignorance of thy buyer take any advantage.

12. Pay the debts which thou oweth: for he who gave thee credit, relieth upon thine honor; and to withhold from him his due, is both mean and unjust.

13. Finally, 0 son of society, examine thy heart, call remembrance to thy aid; and if in any of these things thou hath transgressed, make a speedy reparation, to the utmost of thy power.

CHAPTER XXXII

HOLY INSTRUCTIONS FROM THE PROPHET

CHARITY

1. Happy is the man who hath sown in his breast the seeds of benevolence: the produce thereof shall be charity and love.

2. From the fountain of his heart shall rise rivers of goodness; and the streams shall overflow, for the benefit of mankind.

3. He assisteth the poor in their trouble; he rejoiceth in furthering the prosperity of all men.

4. He censureth not his neighbor; he believeth not the tales of envy and malevolence; neither repeateth he their slanders.

5. He forgiveth the injuries of men, he wipeth them from his remembrance; revenge and malice have no place in his heart.

6. For evil he returneth not evil, he hateth not even his enemies, but requiteth their injustice with a friendly admonition.

7. The griefs and anxieties of men excite his compassion; he endeavoreth to alleviate the weight of their misfortunes, and the pleasure of success rewardeth his labor.

8. He calmeth the fury, he healeth the quarrels of angry men, and preventeth the mischiefs of strife and animosity.

9. He promoteth in his neighborhood peace and good will, and his name is repeated with praise and benedictions.

CHAPTER XXXIII

HOLY INSTRUCTIONS FROM THE PROPHET

GRATITUDE

1. As the branches of a tree return their sap to the root, from whence it arose; as a river poureth its streams to the sea, whence the spring was supplied; so the heart of a grateful man delighteth in returning a benefit recieved.

2. He acknowledgeth his obligation with cheerfulness, he looketh on his benefactor with love and esteem.

3. And if to return it be not in his power, he nourisheth the memory of it in his breast with kindness; he forgetteth it not all the days of his life.

4. The heart of the grateful man is like the clouds of heaven which drops upon the eath, fruits, herbage and flowers; but the heart of the ungrateful is like a desert of sand which swalloweth with greediness the showers that fall, and burieth them in its bosom, and produceth nothing.

5. Envy not thy benefactor, neither strive to conceal the benefit he hath conferred; for though to oblige is better than to be obliged, though the act of generosity commandeth admiration, yet the humility toucheth the heart, and is amiable on the sight both of Allah and man.

6. But receive not a favor from the hand of the proud; to the selfish and avaricious have no obligation; the vanity of pride shall expose thee to shame; the greediness of avarice shall never be satisfied.

CHAPTER XXXIV

HOLY INSTRUCTIONS FROM THE PROPHET

SINCERITY

1. O thou who are enamored with the beauty of Truth, and hast fixed thy heart on the simplicity of her charms, hold fast thy fidelity unto her, and forsake her not; the constancy of thy virtue shall crown thee with honor.

2. The tongue of the sincere is rooted in heart; hypocrisy and deceit have no place in his words.

3. He blusheth at falsehood, and is founded; but in speaking the truth, he hath a steady eye.

4. He supporteth, as a man, the dignity of his character; to the arts of hypocrisy he scorneth to stoop.

5. He is consistent with himself; he is never embarrassed; he hath courage enough for truth; but to lie he is afraid.

6. He is far above the meanness of dissimulation; the words of his mouth are the thoughts of his heart.

7. Yet, with prudence and caution he openeth his lips; he studieth what is right, and speaketh with discretion.

8. He adviseth with friendship; he reproveth with freedom; and whatsoever he promiseth shall surely be performed.

9. But the heart of the hypocrite is hid in his breast; he maketh his words in the semblance of truth, while the business of his life is only to deceive.

10. He laugheth in sorrow, he weepeth in joy; and the words of his mouth have no interpretation.

11. He worketh in the dark as a mole, and fancieth he is safe; but he blundereth into light, and is betrayed and exposed, with dirt on his head.

12. He passeth his days in perpetual constraint; his tongue and heart are forever at variance.

13. He laboreth for the character of a righteous man; and huggeth himself in the thoughts of his cunning.

14. O fool, fool! The pains which thou taketh to hide what thou art, are more than would make thee what thou wouldst seem; and the children of Wisdom shall mock at thy cunning, when in the midst of security, thy disguise is stripped off, and the finger of derision shall point thee to scorn.

CHAPTER XXXV

HOLY INSTRUCTIONS FROM THE PROPHET

RELIGION

1. There is but one Allah, the author, the creator, the governor of the world; almighty , eternal, and incomprehensible.

2. The sun is not Allah, though his noblest image. He enlighteneth the world with his brightness; his warmth giveth life to the products of the earth. Admire him as the creature, the instrument of Allah, but worship him not.

3. To the one who is supreme, most wise and beneficent, and to Him alone, belong worship, adoration, thanks giving and praise.

4. Who hath stretched forth the heavens with His hands, who hath described with his finger the courses of stars.

5. Who setteth bounds to the ocean, that it cannot pass; and saith unto the stormy winds: "Be still."

6. Who shaketh the earth, and the nations tremble; who dareth His lightnings, and the wicked are dismayed.

7. Who calleth forth worlds by the words of His mouth; who smiteth with His arm, and they sink into nothing.

8. O reverence the majesty of the Omnipotent; and tempt not His anger, lest thou be destroyed.

9. The providence of Allah is ever all His works; He ruleth and directeth with infinite wisdom.

10. He hath instituted laws for the government of the world; He hath wonderfully varied them in all beings; and each, by his nature conformeth to His will.

11. In the depth of His mind, He revolveth all knowledge; the secrets of futurity lie open before Him.

12. The thoughts of thy heart are naked to His view; He knoweth thy determination before they are made.

13. With respect to His prescience there is nothing contingent; with respect to his providence there is nothing accidental.

14. Wonderful is He in all His ways; His counsels are inscrutable; the manner of His knowledge transcendeth thy conception.

15. Pay therefore to His wisdom, all honor and veneration; and bow down thyself in humble and submissive obedience to His supreme discretion.

16. The Father is gracious and beneficent; He hath created the world in mercy and love.

17. His creatures of His hand declare His goodness, and their enjoyments speak of His praise; He clothed them with beauty, He supporteth them with food, He preserveth them with pleasure, from generation to generation.

18. If we lift up our eyes to the heavens, His glory shineth forth; if we cast them down on the earth, it is full of His goodness; the hills and the valleys rejoice and sing; fields, rivers, and woods resound His praise.

19. But thee, He hath distinguished with peculiar favor; and exalted thy station above all creatures.

20. But thee, He hath embued thee with reason, to maintain thy dominion; he hath fitted thee with language, to improve thy society; and exalted thy mind with the powers of meditation, to contemplate and adore His inimitable perfections.

21. And in the laws He hath ordained as the rule of life, so kindly hath He united thy duty to thy nature that obedience to His precepts is happiness to thyself.

22. O praise His goodness with songs of thanksgiving, and meditate in silence on the wonders of His love; let thy heart overflow with gratitude and acknowledgment, let the language of thy lips speak praise and adoration, let the actions of thy life show thy love to His law.

23. Allah is just and righteous, and will judge the earth with equity and truth.

24. Hath He established his laws in goodness and mercy, and shall He not punish the transgressors thereof?

25. O think not, bold men, because thy punishment is delayed, that the arm of Allah is weakened; neither flatter thyself with hopes that He winketh at thy doings.

26. His eye pierceth the secrets of every heart, and He rememebereth them forever; He respecteth not the persons or the stations of men.

27. The high and the low, the rich and the poor, the wise and the ignorant, when the soul hath shaken off the cumbrous shackles of this mortal life, shall equality receive, from the sentence of just and everlasting retribution, according to their works.

28. Then shall the wicked tremble and be afraid; but the heart of the righteous shall rejoice in His judgements.

29. O fear Allah, therefore, all the days of thy life, and walk in the paths which He hath opened before thee. Let prudence admonish thee, let temperance restrain, let justice guide thy hand, benevolence warm thy heart, and gratitude to Heaven inspire thee with devotion. These shall give thee happiness in thy present state, and bring thee to the mansions of eternal felicity in the paradise of Allah.

30. This is the true economy of Human Life.

CHAPTER XXXVI

HOLY INSTRUCTIONS FROM THE PROPHET

KNOW THYSELF

1. Weak and ignorant as thou art, O man, humble as thou oughtest to be, O child of the dust, wouldst thou raise thy thoughts to infinite wisdom? Wouldst thou see omnipotence displayed before thee? Contemplate thine frame.

2. Fearfully and wonderfully art thou made; praise therefore thy Creator with awe, and rejoice before Him with reverence.

3. Wherefore of all creatures art thou only erect, but that thou shouldst behold his works? Wherefore art thou to behold, but that thou mayest admire them? Wherefore to admire but that thou mayest adore their and thy Creator?

4. Wherefore is consciousness reposed on thee alone, and whence is it derived to thee?

5. It is not in flesh to think; it is not in bones to reason. The lion knoweth not that worms shall eat him; the ox perceiveth not that he is fed for slaughter.

6. Something is added to thee, unlike to what thou seest; something informs the clay; higher than all is the object of thy senses. Behold, what is it?

7. The body remaineth perfect after it is fled; therefore it is no part of it; it is immaterial, therefore it is eternal; it is free to act; therefore it is accountable for its actions.

8. Knoweth the ass the use of food, because his teeth mow down the herbage? Or standeth the crocodile erect, although his backbone is as straight as thine?

9. Allah formed thee as He formed these; after them all wert thou created; superiority and command were given thee over all, and of His own breath did he communicate to thee the principle of knowledge.

10. Know thyself and the pride of His creation, the line uniting divinity and matter; behold a part of Allah Himself within thee; remember thine own dignity; nor dare descend to evil or to meanness.

11. Who planted terror in the tail of the serpent? Who clothed the neck of the horse with thunder? Even He who hath instructed thee to crush the one under thy feet, and to tame the other to thy purpose.

CHAPTER XXXVII

HOLY INSTRUCTIONS FROM THE PHOPHET

THE BREATH OF HEAVEN

1. Vaunt not thy body; because it was first formed; nor of thy brain, because therein thy soul resideth. Is not the master of the house more honorable than its walls?

2. The ground must be prepared before corn be planted; the potter must build his furnace before he can make his porcelain.

3. As the breath of Heaven sayeth unto the waters of the deep; "This way shall thy billows roll, and no other; thus high, and no higher shall they raise their fury"; so let thy spirit, 0 man, actuate and direct thy flesh; so let it repress its wilderness.

5. Thy body is as the globe of the earth; thy bones the pillars that sustain it on its basis.

6. As the ocean giveth rise to springs, whose waters return again into its bosom through the rivers; so runneth thy life from thy outwards, and so runneth it into its place again.

7. Do not both retain their course forever? Behold, the same Allah ordained them.

8. Is not thy nose the channel to perfumes, thy mouth the path to delicacies.

9. Are not thine eyes the sentinels that watch for thee? Yet how often are they unable to distinguish truth from error?

10. Keep thy soul in moderation; teach thy spirit to be attentive to its good; so shall these its ministers be always to thee conveyances of truth.

11. Thine hand, is it not a miracle? Is there in the creation aught like unto it? Wherefore was it given thee, but that thou mightest stretch it out to the assistance of thy brother?

12. Why of all things living are thou alone made capable of blushing? The world shall read thy shame upon thy face; therefore do nothing shameful.

13. Fear and dismay, which robs thy countenance of its ruddy splendor, avoid guilt, and thou shalt know that fear is beneath thee, that dismay is unnamely.

14. Wherefore to thee alone speaks shadows in the vision of the pillow? Reverence them; for know that dreams are from on high.

15. Thou man alone canst speak. Wonder at thy glorious prerogative; and pay to Him who gave it to thee a rational and welcome praise, teaching thy children wisdom, instructing the offspring of thy loins in piety.

CHAPTER XXXVIII

HOLY INSTRUCTIONS FROM THE PROPHET

THE SOUL OF MAN

1. The blessing, 0 man, of thy external part is health, vigor and proportion. The greatest of these is health. What health is to the body even that is honesty to the soul.

2. That thou hast a soul is of all knowledge the most certain of all truths the most plain unto thee. Be meek, be grateful for it. Seek not to know it perfectly. It is inscrutable.

3. Thinking, understanding, reasoning, willing, call not these the soul. They are its actions, but they are not its essence.

4. Raise it not too high, that thou be not despised. Be not thou like unto those who fall by climbing; neither debase it to the sense of brutes, nor be thou like to the horse and the mule, in whom there is no understanding.

5. Search it by its faculties: know it by its virtues. They are more in number than the hairs of thy head; the stars of heaven are not to be counted with them.

6. Think not with Arabia, that one soul is parted among all men; neither believe thou with the sons of Egypt, that every man hath many; know, that as thy heart, so also thy soul is one.

7. Doth not the sun harden the clay? Doth it not also soften the wax? As it is one sun that worketh both, even so it is one soul willeth contraries.

8. As the moon retaineth her nature, though darkness spread itself before her face as a curtain; so the soul remaineth perfect, even in the bosom of a fool.

9. She is immortal; she is unchangeable; she is alike in all. Health calleth her forth to show her loveliness, and application anointeth her with the oil of wisdom.

10. Although she shall live after thee, think not she was born before thee. She was created with thy flesh, and formed with thy brain.

11. Justice could not give her to thee exalted by virtues, nor mercy deliver her to thee deformed by vices. These must be thine, and thou must answer for them.

12. Suppose not death can shield thee from examination; think not corruption can hide thee from inquiry. He who formed thee of thou knowest not what, can he not raise thee from thou knowest not what again?

13. Perceiveth not the cock the hour of midnight? Exalteth he not his voice to tell thee it is morning? Knoweth not the dog the footsteps of his master? Flieth not the wounded goat unto the herb that healeth him? Yet when these die, their spirit returneth to dust; thine alone surviveth.

14. Envy not to these their senses, because quicker than thine own. Learn that the advantage lieth not in possessing good things, but in the knowing to use them.

15. Hadst thou the ear of the stag, or were thine eyes as strong and piercing as the eagles; didst thou equal the hound in smell, or could the ape resign to thee his taste, or could the tortoise her feeling; yet without reason what would they avail thee? Perish not all these like their kindred?

16. Hath any one of them the gift of speech? Can any say unto thee, "Therefore did I do?"

17. The lips of the wise are as the doors of a cabinet; no sooner are they opened but treasures are poured out before thee.

18. Like unto trees of gold arranged in beds of silver are wise sentences uttered in due season.

19. Canst thou think too greatly of thy soul? Or can too much be said in its praise? It is the image of Him who gave it.

20. Remember thou its dignity forever; forget not how great a talent is committed to thy charge.

21. Whatsoever may do good, may also do harm. Beware that thou direct its course to virtue.

22. Think not that thou canst lose her in a crowd; suppose not that thou canst bury her in thy closet. Action is her delight, and she will not be withheld from it.

23. Her motion is perpetual; her attempts are universal; her agility is not to be suppressed. Is it at the uttermost parts of the earth? She will have it. Is it beyond the regions of the stars? Yet will her eye discover it, Inquiry is her delight. As one who traverseth the burning sands, in search of water, so is the soul that thirsteth after knowledge.

24. Guard her for she is rash; restrain her, for she is irregular; correct her, for she is outrageous; more supple is she than water, more flexible than wax, more yielding than air. Is there aught that can bind her?

25. As a sword in the hand of a mad man, even so is the soul to him who wanteth discretion.

26. The end of her search is truth; her means to discover it are reason and experience. But are not these weak, uncertain and fallacious? How then shall she attain unto it?

27. General opinion is no proof of truth, for the generality of men are ignorant.

28. Perception of thyself, the knowledge of Him who create thee, the sense of worship thou owest unto Him. Are not these plain before thy face? And, behold! What is there more that men needeth to know?

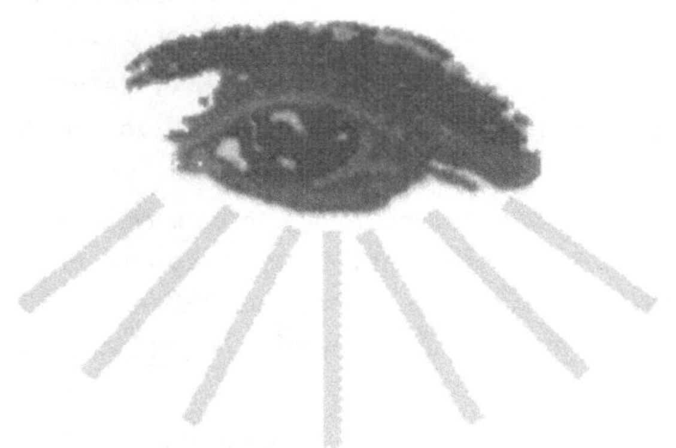

CHAPTER XXXIX

HOLY INSTRUCTIONS FROM THE PROPHET

PINNACLE OF WISDOM

1. As the eye of the morning to the lark, as the shade of the evening to the owl, as honey to the bee, or as the carcass to the vulture even such is life unto the heart of man.

2. Though bright, it dazzleth not; though obscure, it displeaseth not; though sweet, it cloyeth not; though corrupt, it forbiddeth not, yet who is he that knoweth its true value?

3. Learn to esteem as thou ought; then art thou near the pinnacle of wisdom.

4. Think not, with the fool, that nothing is more valuable; nor believe, with the pretended wise, that thou oughtest to condemn it. Love it not thyself, but for the good it may be of to others.

5. Gold cannot buy it for thee neither mines of diamonds purchase back the moment thou hast now lost it. Employ the succeeding ones in virtue.

6. Say not that it were best not to have been born: or, if born that it has been best to die early; neither dare thou to ask of thy Creator, "Where has been the evil, had I not existed?" Good is thy power, the want of good is evil; and if thy question be just, lo, it condemneth thee.

7. Would the fish swallow the bait if he knew the hook were hidden therein? Would the lion enter the toils if he saw they were prepared for him? So neither, were the soul to perish with this clay, neither would a merciful Father have created him; know hence thou shalt live afterwards.

8. As the bird, enclosed in the cage before he seeth it, yet teareth not his flesh against its sides; so neither labor thou vainly to run the state thou art in, but know it is alloted thee, and be content with it.

9. Though its ways are uneven, yet they are not all painful. Accommodate thyself to all; and where there is the least appearance of evil, suspect the greatest danger.

10. When thy bed is straw, thou sleepest in security; but when thou stretcheth thyself on roses beware of the thorns.

11. A good death is better than an evil life; strive therefore, to live as long as thou oughtest, not as long as thou canst. While thy life is to others worth more than thy death, it is thy duty to preserve it.

12. Complain not, with the fool, of the shortness of thy time: remember, with thy days thy cares are shortened.

13. Take from the period of thy life the useless part of it, and what remaineth?

14. Take off the time of thine infancy, thy second infancy of age, thy sleep, thy thoughtless hours, thy days of sickness; and, even at thy fulness of years, how few seasons hast truly numbered!

15. He who gave thee life as a blessing, shortened it to make it even more so.

16. To what end would longer life have served thee? Wishest thou to have had an opportunity of more vices? As to the good, will not He who limited thy span, be satisfied with the fruits of it?

17. To what end, O child of sorrow, wouldst thou live longer. To breathe, to eat, to see the world? All this thou hast done often already. Too frequent repetition, is it not tiresome? Or is it not superfluous?

18. Wouldst thou improve thy wisdom and thy virtue? Alas! What art thou to know? Or who is it that shall teach thee? Badly thou employest the little thou hast; dare not, therefore, to complain that the more is not given thee.

19. Repine not at thy want of knowledge; it must perish within the grave. Be honest here, thou shalt be wise hereafter.

20. Say not unto the crow, "Why numberest thou seven times thy Lord?" or to the fawn, "Why art thine eyes to see my offspring an hundred generations?" Are these to be compared with thee in the abuse of life?

21. Are they riotous? Are they cruel? Are they ungrateful? Learn from them, rather, that innocence of manners are the paths of good old age.

22. Knowest thou to employ life better than these? Then less of it may suffice thee.

23. Man, who dares enslave the world, when he knows he can enjoy his tyranny but for a moment, what would he not aim at, if he were immortal.

24. Enough hath thou of life, but thou regardest it not; thou are not in want of it, O man, but thou art prodigal; thou threwest it lightly away, as if thou hadst more than enough; and yet thou repinest that it is not gathered again unto thee. Know, that it is not abundance which maketh rich, but Economy.

25. The wise continueth to live from his first period; the fool is always beginning.

26. Labor not after riches first, and think thou wilt afterwards enjoy them. He who neglecteth the present moment, throweth away all that he hath. As the arrow passeth through the heart while the warrior knew not that it was coming; so shall his life be taken away, before he knoweth that he hath it.

27. What then is life, that man should desire it? What, breathing that he should covet it?

28. Is it not a scene of delusion, a series of misadventures, a pursuit of evils linked on all sides together? In the beginning, it is ignorance, pain is in its middle; and its end is sorrow.

29. As one wave pusheth on another, till both are involved in that behind them; even so succeedeth evil to evil, in the life of man; the greatest and the present swallow up the lesser and the past. Our terrors are real evils; our expectations look forward into impossibilities.

30. Fools, to dread as mortals, and to desire as if immortal!

31. What part of life is it that we should wish to remain with us? Is it youth? Can we be in love with outrage, licentiousness, and temerity? Is it age? Then we are fond of infirmities.

32. It is said, grey hairs are revered, and length of days an honor. Virtue can add reverence to the bloom of youth; and without it, age plants more wrinkles in the soul than on the forehead.

33. Is age respected because it hateth riot? What justice is in this when it is not age that despiseth pleasure, but pleasure that despiseth age.

34. Be virtuous while thou are young, so shall thine age be honored.

CHAPTER XL
HOLY INSTRUCTIONS FROM THE PROPHET
THE INSTABILITY OF MAN

1. Inconstancy is powerful in the heart of man; Intemperance swayeth it whither it will; Despair engrosseth much of it; and Fear proclaimeth: "Behold, I sit unrivalled therein," but Vanity is beyond them all.

2. Weep not therefore at the calamities of the human state; rather laugh at its follies. In the hands of the man addicted to vanity, life then is but the shadow of a dream.

3. The hero, the most renowned of human character, what is he, but the bubble of this weakness. The public is unstable and ungrateful. Why should the man of wisdom endanger himself for fools?

4. The man who neglecteth his present concerns, to revolve how he will behave when greater, feedeth himself with wind, while his bread is eaten by another.

5. Act as becometh thee in thy present station, and in more exalted ones thy face shall not be ashamed.

6. What blindeth the eye, or what hideth the heart of a man from himself, like Vanity? Lo, when thou seest not thyself, then others discover thee, most plainly.

7. As the tulip that is gaudy without smell, conspicuous without use; so is the mail who sitteth himself up so high, and hot not merit.

8. The heart of the vain is troubled while it seemeth content; his cares are greater than his pleasures.

9. His solicitude cannot rest with his bones, the grave is not deep enough to hide it; he extendeth his thoughts beyond his being; he bespeaketh praise; to be paid when he is gone; but whosoever promiseth it, deceiveth him.

10. As the man who engageth his wife to remain in widowhood, that she disturb not his soul; so is he who expecteth that his praise shall reach his ears beneath the earth, or cherish his heart in its shroud.

11. Do well whilst thou liveth; but regard not what is said of it. Content thyself with deserving praise, and thy posterity shall rejoice in hearing it.

12. As the butterfly who seeth not his own colors, as the jasmine which feeleth not the scent it casteth around it; so is the man who appeareth gay, and biddeth others to take note of it.

13. "To what purpose," saith he, "is my vesture of gold, to what end are my tables filled with dainties, if no eye gaze upon them, if the world knows it not?" Give thy raiment to the naked, and thy food unto the hungry; so shalt thou be praised, and feel that thou deserveth it.

14. Why bestoweth thou in every man the flattery of unmeaning words? Thou knowest, when returned thee, thou regardest it not. He knoweth he lieth unto thee, yet he knoweth thou will thank him for it. Speak in sincerity, and thou wilt hear with instruction.

15. The vain delighteth to speak of himself; but he seeth not that others like not to hear him.

16. If he hath done anything worth praise, if he possesseth that which is worthy of admiration, his joy is to proclaim it, his pride to hear it reported. The desire of such a man defeateth itself. Men say not: "Behold he hath done it," or "See, he possesseth it," but "Mark how proud he is of it."

17. The heart of man cannot attend at once to too many things. He who fixeth his soul on show, loseth reality. He pursueth bubbles, which break in their flight, while he treads to earth what would him honor.

CHAPTER XLI

HOLY INSTRUCTIONS FROM THE PROPHET

INCONSTANCY

1. Nature urgeth thee to inconstancy, 0 man! Therefore guard thyself at all times against, it.

2. Thou art, from the womb of thy mother, various and wavering, from the loins of thy father inheriteth thou instability. How then shalt thou be firm ?

3. Those who gave thee a body, furnished it with weakness; but He who gave thee a soul, armed thee. with resolution. Employ it, and thou art wise be wise, and thou art happy.

4. Let him who doeth well, beware how he boasteth of it, for rarely is it of his own will.

5. Is not the event of an impulse, from without born of uncertainty enforced by accident, dependent on somewhat else? To thee, and to accident, is due the praise.

6. Beware of irresolution in the intent of thy actions; beware of instability in the execution; so shalt thou triumph over two great failings of thy nature.

7. What reproacheth reason more than to act contrarieties? What can suppress the tendencies to these, but firmness of mind?

8. The inconstant feeleth that he changeth, but he knoweth not why; he seeth that he escapeth from himself, but he perceiveth not how. Be thou incapable of change, in that which is right, and men will rely upon thee.

9. Establish unto thyself principles of action, and see that thou ever act according to them.

10. So shall thy passions have no rule over thee; so shall thy constancy ensure unto thee the good thou possesseth, and drive from thy door misfortune. Anxiety and disappointment shall be strangers to thy gates.

11. Suspect not evil in anyone until thou seeth it; when thou seeth, forget it not.

12. Who so hath been an enemy, cannot be a friend; for man mendeth not his faults.

13. How should his actions be right, who hath no rule of his life? Nothing can be just which proceedeth not from reason.

14. The inconstant hath no peace in his soul; neither can be at ease whom he concerneth himself with.

15. His life is unequal; his motions are irregular; his soul changeth with the weather.

16. Today he loveth thee, tomorrow thou art detested by him; and why? Himself knoweth not wherefore he now hateth.

17. Today he is the tyrant, tomorrow thy servant is less humble; and why? He who is arrogant without power, will be servile while there is no subjection.

18. Today he is profuse, tomorrow he grudgeth unto his mouth that which it should eat. Thus it is with him who knoweth not moderation.

19. Who shall say of the camelion: "He is black," when, the moment after the verdure of the grass, overspreadeth him?

20. Who shall say of the inconstant: "He is joyful," when his next breath shall be spent in sighing?

21. What is the life of such a man, but the phantom of a dream? In the morning he riseth happy, at noon he is on the rack; this hour he is a god, the next below a worm; one moment he laugheth, the next he weepeth; he now willeth, in an instant he willeth not, and in another he knoweth not whether he willeth or not.

22. Yet neither ease nor pain have fixed themselves on him; neither is he waxed greater, or become less; neither hath he had cause for laughter, or reason for his sorrow; therefore shall none of them abide with him.

23. The happiness of the inconstant is as a palace built on the surface of the sand; the blowing of the wind carrieth away its foundation; What wonder then that it falleth?

24. But what exalted form is this, that hitherward directs its even, its uninterrupted course - whose foot is on earth, whose head is above the clouds?

25. On his brow sitteth majesty; steadiness is in his port; and in his heart reigneth tranquility.

26. Though obstacles appear in his way, he deigneth not to look down upon them; though heaven and earth oppose his passage; he proceedeth.

27. The mountains sink beneath his tread; the waters of the ocean are dried up under the sole of his foot.

28. The tiger throweth herself across his way in vain; the spots of the leopard glow against him unregarded.

29. He marcheth through the embattled legions; with his hands he putteth aside the terrors of death.

30. Storms roar against his shoulders, but are not able to shake them; the thunder bursteth over his head in vain; the lightning serveth but to show the glories of his countenance.

31. His name is Resolution! He cometh from the utmost part of the earth; he seeth happiness afar off before him; his eye discovereth her temple beyond the limits of the pole.

32. He walketh up to it, he entereth boldly, and he remaineth there forever.

33. Establish thy heart, O man, in that which is right; and then know, the greatest of human is to be immutable.

CHAPTER XLII

HOLY INSTRUCTIONS FROM THE PROPHET

WEAKNESS

1. Vain and inconstant as thou art, 0 child of imperfection, how canst thou be weak? Is not inconstancy connected with frailty? Can there be vanity without infirmity? Avoid the danger of the one, and thou shalt escape the mischiefs of the other.

2. Wherein art thou most weak? In that wherein thou seemest most strong; in that wherein most thou glorieth; even in possessing the things which thou hast; in using the good that is about thee.

3. Art not thy desires also frail? Or knoweth thou even what it is thou wouldst wish? When thou hast obtained what most thou soughteth after, behold, it contenteth thee not.

4. Wherefore loseth the pleasure that is before thee its relish? And why appeareth that which is yet to come the sweeter? Because thou art wearied with the good of this, because thou knoweth not the evil of that which is not with thee. Know that to be content, is to be happy.

5. Couldst thou choose for thyself, would thy Creator lay before thee all that thy heart could ask for, would happiness then remain with thee, or would joy always dwell in thy gates?

6. Alas! Thy weakness forbiddeth it; thy infirmity declareth against it. Variety is to thee in the place of pleasure; but that which permanently delighteth, must be permanent.

7. When that is gone, thou repenteth the loss of it; though, while it was with thee, thou despiseth it.

8. That which succeedeth it, hath no more pleasure to thee; and thou afterwards quarreleth with thyself for preferring it; behold the only circumstances in which thou arrest not!

9. Is there any thing in which thy weakness appeareth more, than in desiring things? It is in the possessing, and in the using of them.

10. Good things cease to be good in our enjoyment of them. What nature meant pure sweets, are sources of bitterness to us, from our delights arise pain, from our joys, sorrow.

11. Be moderate in the enjoyment, and it shall remain in thy possession; let thy joy be founded on reason, and to its end shall sorrow be a stranger.

12. The delights of love are ushered in by sighs, and they terminate in languishment and dejection. The objects thou burnedeth for, nauseates with satiety; and no sooner hast thou possessed it, but thou art weary of its presence.

13. Join esteem to thy admiration, unite friendship with the love; so shalt thou find in the end content so absolute, that it surpasseth raptures, tranquility more worth than ecstasy.

14. Allah hath given thee no good, without its admixture of evil; but he hath given thee also the means of throwing off the evil from it.

15. As joy is not without its alloy of pain, so neither is sorrow without its portion of pleasure. Joy and grief, though unlike, are united. Our own choice only can give them to us entirely.

16. Melancholy itself often giveth delight, and the extremity of joys are mingled with tears.

17. The best things in the hands of a fool may be turned to his destruction; and out of the worst, the wise will find means of good.

18. So blended is weakness in thy nature, 0 man, that thou hast not strength either to be good nor to be evil, entirely. Rejoice that thou canst not excel in evil, and let the good that is within thy reach content thee.

19. The virtues are allotted to various stations. Seek not after impossiblities, nor grieve that thou canst not possess them all.

20. Wouldst thou at once have the liberality of the rich, and the contentment of the poor? Shall the wife of thy bosom be despised because she showeth not the virtues of the widow?

21. If thy father sink before thee in the divisions of thy country, can at once thy justice destroy him, and thy duty save his life?

22. If thou behold thy brother in the agonies of slow death, is not mercy to put a period to his life? And is it not also death to be his murderer?

23. Truth is but one; thy doubts are of thine own raising. He who made virtues what they are, planted in thee a knowledge of their pre-eminence. Act as thy soul dictates to thee, and the end shall be always right.

CHAPTER XLIII

HOLY INSTRUCTIONS FROM THE PROPHET

THE INSUFFICIENCY OF KNOWLEDGE

1. If there is anything lovely, if there is anything desirable, if there is anything within the reach of man that is worthy of praise, is it not knowledge? And yet who is it that attaineth it?

2. The statesman proclaimeth that he hath it; the ruler of the people claimeth the praise of it -- but findeth the subject that he posssesseth it?

3. Evil is not requisite to man; neither can vice be necessary to be tolerated; yet how many evils are permitted by the connivance of the laws; how many crimes committed by the decree of the council!

4. But be wise, 0 ruler, and learn, 0 thou that are to command the nations! One crime authorized by thee is worse than the escape of ten from punishment.

5. When the people are numerous, when thy sons increase about thy table; sendest thou them not out to slay the innocent, and to fall before the sword of him whom they have not offended?

6. If the objects of thy desire demanding the lives of a thousand sayeth thou not: "I will have it." Surely thou forgetteth that He who created thee, created also these; and that their blood is as rich as thine ?

7. Sayeth thou, that justice cannot be executed without wrong? Surely thine own words condemn thee.

8. Thou who flattereth with false hopes the criminal that he may confess his guilt, art not thou unto him a criminal? Or art thou guiltless, because he cannot punish it?

9. When thou commandest to the torture him whom is but suspected of ill, dareth thou to remember, that thou mayest rack the innocent?

10. Is thy purpose answered by the event? Is thy soul satisfied with his confession? Pain will enforce him to say what is not, as easy as what is, and anguish hath caused innocence to accuse herself.

11. That thou mayest not kill him without cause, thou dost worse than kill him; that thou mayest prove if he be guilty, thou detsroyeth him innocent.

12. O blindness to all truth! O insufficience of the wisdom of the wise! Know, when thy judge shall bid thee account for this, thou shalt wish ten thousand guilty to have gone free, rather than one innocent to stand forth against thee.

13. Insufficient as thou art to the maintenance of justice, how shalt thou arrive at the knowledge of truth? How shalt thou ascend to the footstep of her throne?

14. As the owl is blinded by the radiance of the sun, so shall the brightness of her countenance dazzle thee in thy approaches.

15. If thou wouldst mount onto her throne, first bow thyself at her footstool. if thou wouldst arrive at the knowledge of her, first inform thyself of thine own ignorance.

16. More worth is she than pearls, therefore seek her carefully; the emerald and the sapphire, and the ruby are as dirt beneath her feet; therefore pursue her manfully.

17. The way to her is labor; attention is the pilot that must conduct thee into her port. But weary not on the way; for when art arrived at her, the toil shall be to thee for pleasure.

18. Say not unto thyself: "Behold, truth breedeth hatred, and I will avoid it; dissimulation raiseth friends, and I will follow it." Are not the enemies made by truth, better than the friends obtained by flattery?

19. Naturally doth man desire the truth; yet, when it is before him, he will not apprehend it; and if it force itself upon him, he is not offended at it.

20. The fault is not in truth, for that is amiable; but the weakness of man beareth not its splendor.

21. Wouldst thou see thine insufficence more plainly? View at thy devotions! To what end was religion instituted, but to teach thee thine infirmities, to remind thee of thy weakness, to show thee that from Heaven alone art thou to hope for good?

22. Doth it not remind thee that thou art dust? Doth it not tell thee that thou art ashes? And behold repentance, is it not frailty?

23. When thou givest an oath; when thou swearest thou wilt not deceive; behold it spreadeth shame upon thy face, and upon the face of him that receiveth it. Learn to be just, and repentance may be forgotten; learn to be honest, and oaths are unnecessary.

24. The shorter follies are, the better; say not therefore to thyself: "I will not play the fool by halves."

25. He that heareth his own faults with patience, shall reprove another with boldness.

26. He that giveth a denial with reason, shall suffer a repulse with moderation.

27. If thou art suspected, answer with freedom. Whom should suspicion affright, except the guilty?

28. The tender of heart is turned from his purpose by supplications, the proud is rendered more obstinate by entreaty; the sense of thine insufficience commandeth thee to hear; but to be just, thou must hear without thy passions.

CHAPTER XLIV

HOLY INSTRUCTIONS FROM THE PROPHET

MISERY

1. Feeble and insufficient as thou art, O man, in good; frail and inconsistent as thou art in pleasure; yet there is a thing in which thou art strong and unshaken. Its name is Misery.

2. It is the character of thy being, the prerogative of thy nature; in thy breast alone, it resideth; without thee, there is nothing of it. And behold, what is its source, but thine own passions?

3. He who gave thee these, gave thee also reason to subdue them; exert it, and thou shall trample them under thy feet!

4. Thine entrance into the world, is it not shameful? Thy destruction, is it not glorious-- Lo! men adorn the instruments of death with gold and gems and wear them above their garments.

5. He who begetteth a man, hideth his face; but he who killeth a thousand is honored.

6. Know thou, notwithstanding, that in this is error. Custom cannot alter the nature of truth, neither can the opinion of man destroy justice; the glory and the shame are misplaced.

7. There is but one way for a man to be produced; there are a thousand by which he may be destroyed.

8. There is no praise or honor to him who giveth being to another; but triumphs and empire are the rewards of murder.

9. Yet he who hath many children, hath many blessings; and he who hath taken away the life of another, shall not enjoy his own.

10. While the savage curseth the birth of his son, and blesseth the death of his father, doth he not call himself a monster?

11. The greatest of all human ills is sorrow; too much of this thou art born into; add not unto it by thy own perverseness.

12. Grief is natural to thee, and is always about thee; pleasure is a stranger and visiteth thee by times; use well thy reason, and sorrow will be cast behind thee; be prudent, and the visits of joy shall remain long with thee.

13. Every part of thy frame is capable of sorrow, but few and narrow are the paths that lead to delight.

14. Pleasures can be admitted only simply, but pains rush in a thousand at a time.

15. As the blaze of straw fadeth as soon as it is kindled, so passeth away the brightness of joy, and thou knoweth not what become of it.

16. Sorrow is frequent, pleasure is rare; pain cometh of itself; delight must be purchased; grief is unmixed, but joy wanteth not its alloy of bitterness.

17. As the soundest health is less perceived than the lightest malady, so the highest joy toucheth us less deep than the smallest sorrow.

18. We are in love with anguish; we often fly from pleasure; when we purchase it, costeth it not more than it is worth?

19. Reflection is the business of man; sense of his state is his first duty; but who remembereth himself a boy? Is it not in mercy, then, that sorrow is allotted unto us?

20. Man forseeth the evil that is to come; he remembereth it when it is past; he considereth not that the thought of affliction woundeth deeper than the affliction itself. Think not of thy pain, but when it is upon thee, and thou shalt avoid what most hurt thee.

21. He who weepeth before he needeth, weepeth more than he needeth; and why, but that he loveth weeping?

22. The stag weepeth not till the spear is lifted against him; nor do the tears of the beaver fall, till the hound is ready to seize him; man anticipateth death by the apprehension of it: and the fear is greater misery than the event itself.

23. Be always prepared to give an account of thine action; and the best death is that which is least premeditated.

CHAPTER XLV

THE DIVINE ORIGIN OF THE ASIATIC NATIONS

1. The fallen sons and daughters of the Asiatic Nation of North America need to learn to love instead of hate; and to know their higher self and lower self. This is the uniting of the Holy Koran of Mecca, for teaching and instructing all Moorish Americans, etc.

2. The key of civilization was and is in the hands of the Asiatic nations. The Moorish, who were ancient Moabites, and the founders of the Holy City of Mecca.

3. The Egyptians who were the Hamathites, and of a direct descendant of Mizraim, the Arabians, the seed of Hagar, Japanese and Chinese.

4. The Hindoos of India, the descendants of the ancient Canaanites, Hittites, and Moabites of the land of Canaan.

5. The Asiatic nations of North, South, and Central America: the Moorish Americans and Mexicans of North America, Brazilians, Argentinians and Chilians in South America.

6. Columbians, Nicaraguans, and the natives of San Salvador in Central America, etc. All of these are Moslems.

7. The Turks are the true descendants of Hagar, who are the chief protectors of the Islamic Creed of Mecca; beginning from Mohammed the First, the founding of the uniting of Islam, by the command of the great universal God--Allah.

CHAPTER XLVI

THE BEGINNING OF CHRISTIANITY

1. The foundation of Christianity began in Rome. The Roman nations founded the first Church, of whom crucified Jesus of Nazareth for seeking to redeem His people from under the Roman yoke and law.

2. Jesus himself was of the true blood of the ancient Canaanites and Moabites and the inhabitants of Africa.

3. Seeking to redeem His people in those days from the pressure of the pale skin nations of Europe, Rome crucified Him according to their law.

4. Then Europe had peace for a long time until Mohammed the First came upon the scene and fulfilled the works of Jesus of Nazareth.

5. The holy teaching of Jesus was to the common people, to redeem them from under the great pressure of the hands of the unjust. That the rulers and the rich would not oppress the poor. Also that the lion and the lamb may lay down together and neither would be harmed when morning came.

6. These teachings were not accepted by the rulers, neither by the rich; because they loved the principles of the ten commandments.

7. Through the ten commandments the rulers and the rich live, while the poor suffer and die.

8. The lamb is the poor people, the lion is the rulers and the rich, and through Love, Truth, Peace, Freedom, and Justice all men are one and equal to seek their own destiny; and to worship under their own vine and fig tree. After the principles of the holy and divine laws of their forefathers.

9. All nations of the earth in these modern days are seeking peace, but there is but one true and divine way that peace may be obtained in these days, and it is through Love, Truth, Peace, Freedom, and Justice being taught universally to all nations, in all lands.

CHAPTER XLVII

EGYPT, THE CAPITAL EMPIRE OF THE DOMINION OF AFRICA

1. The inhabitants of Africa are the descendants of the ancient Canaanites from the land of Canaan.

2. Old man Cush and his family are the first inhabitants of Africa who came from the land of Canaan.

3. His father Ham and his family were second. Then came the word Ethiopia, which means the demarcation line of the dominion of Amexem, the first true and divine name of Africa. The dividing of the land between the father and the son.

4. The dominion of Cush, North-East and South-East Africa and North-West and South-West was his father's dominion of Africa.

5. In later years many of their bretheren from Asia and the Holy Lands joined them.

6. The Moabites from the land of Moab who received permission from the Pharaohs of Egypt to settle and inhabit North-West Africa; they were the founders and are the true possessors of the present Moroccan Empire. With their Canaanite, Hittite, and Amorite bretheren who sojourned from the land of Canaan seeking new homes.

7. Their dominion and inhabitation extended from North-East and South-West Africa, across great Atlantis even unto the present North, South, and Central America and also Mexico and the Atlantis Islands; before the great earthquake, which caused the great Atlantic Ocean.

8. The River Nile was dredged and made by the ancient Pharaohs of Egypt, in order to trade with the surrounding kingdoms. Also the Niger river was dredged by the great Pharaoh of Egypt in those ancient days for trade, and it extends eastward from the River Nile, westward across the great Atlantic. It was used for trade and transportation.

9. According to all true and divine records of the human race there is no negro, black, or colored race attached to the human family, because all the inhabitants of Africa were and are of the human race, descendants of the ancient Canaanite nation from the holy land of Canaan.

10. What your ancient forefathers were, you are today without doubt or contradiction.

11. There is no one who is able to change man from the descendant nature of his forefathers; unless his power extends beyond the great universal Creator Allah Himself.

12. These holy and divine laws are from the Prophet, Noble Drew Ali, the founder of the uniting of the Moorish Science Temple of America.

13. These laws are to be strictly preserved by the members of all the Temples, of the Moorish Science Temple of America. That they will learn to open their meeting and guide it according to the principles of Love, Truth, Peace, Freedom and Justice.

14. Every subordinate Temple of the Grand-Major Temple is to form under the covenant of Love, Truth, Peace, Freedom and Justice; and to create their own laws and customs, in conjunction with the laws of the Holy Prophet and the Grand Temple. I, the Prophet, Noble Drew Ali, was sent by the great God, Allah, to warn all Asiatics of America to repent from their sinful ways; before that great and awful day that is sure to come.

15. The time has come when every nation must worship under its own vine and fig tree, and every tongue must confess his own.

16. Through sin and disobedience every nation has suffered slavery, due to the fact that they honored not the creed and principles of their forefathers.

17. That is why the nationality of the Moors was taken away from them in 1774 and the word negro, black and colored, was given to the Asiatics of America who were of Moorish descent, because they honored not the principles of their mother and father, and strayed after the gods of Europe of whom they knew nothing.

CHAPTER XLVIII

THE END OF TIME AND THE FULFILLING OF THE PROPHESIES

1. The last Prophet in these days is Noble Drew Ali, who was prepared divinely in due time by Allah to redeem men from their sinful ways; and to warn them of the great wrath which is sure to come upon the earth.

2. John the Baptist was the forerunner of Jesus in those days, to warn and stir up the nation and prepare them to receive the divine creed which was to be taught by Jesus.

3. In these modern days there came a forerunner of Jesus, who was divinely prepared by the great God-Allah and his name is Marcus Garvey, who did teach and warn the nations of the earth to prepare to meet the coming Prophet; who was to bring the true and divine Creed of Islam, and his name is Noble Drew Ali who was prepared and sent to this earth by Allah, to teach the old time religion and the everlasting gospel to the sons of men. That every nation shall and must worship under their own vine and fig tree, and return to their own and be one with their Father God-Allah.

4. The Moorish Science Temple of America is a lawfully chartered and incorporated organization. Any subordinate Temple that desires to receive a charter; the prophet has them to issue to every state throughout the United States, etc.

5. That the world may hear and know the truth, that among the descendants of Africa there is still much wisdom to be learned in these days for the redemption of the sons of men under Love, Truth, Peace, Freedom, and Justice.

6. We, as a clean and pure nation descended from the inhabitants of Africa, do not desire to amalgamate or marry into the families of the pale skin nations of Europe. Neither serve the gods of their religion, because our forefathers are the true and divine founders of the first religious creed, for the redemption and salvation of mankind on earth.

7. Therefore we are returning the Church and Christianity back to the European Nations, as it was prepared by their forefathers for their earthly salvation.

8. While we, the Moorish Americans are returning to Islam, which was founded by our forefathers for our earthly and divine salvation.

9. The covenant of the great God-Allah: "Honor they father and they mother that thy days may be longer upon the earth land, which the Lord thy God, Allah hath given thee!"

10. Come all ye Asiatics of America and hear the truth about your nationality and birthrights, because you are not negroes. Learn of your forefathers ancient and divine Creed. That you will learn to love instead of hate.

11. We are trying to uplift fallen humanity. Come and link yourselves with the families of nations. We honor all the true and divine prophets.

II. Mysteries of the Silent Brotherhood of the East a.k.a. The Red Book a.k.a. Sincerity

Noble Drew Ali, Prophet. *Mysteries of the Silent Brotherhood of the East.* Redondo Beach, CA: Califa Media, 2014

Chapter I

Life and Works of Jesus in Egypt and India

1. And Jesus came to Egypt Land and all was well. He tarried not upon the coast; he went at once to Zoan, home of Elihu and Salome, who five and twenty years before, had taught his mother in their sacred school.

2. And there was joy when met these three. When last the son of Mary saw these sacred groves, he was a babe.

3. And now, a man had grown strong by buffetings of every kind, a teacher who had stirred the multitudes in many lands.

4. And Jesus told the aged teachers all about his life, about his journey in foreign lands, about the meetings with masters, and about his kind receptions by the multitudes.

5. Elihu and Salome hears this story with delight; they lifted up their eyes to heaven and said"

6. "Our Father Allah, let now thy servants go in peace; for we have seen the glory of the Lord"

7. "And we have talked with him the messenger of Love and of the Covenant of Peace on earth and good will to men."

8. "Through Him shall all the Nations of the earth be blessed through Him, Immanuel."

9. And Jesus stayed in Zoan many days; and then he went forth unto the City of the Sun, that men call Heliopolis, and sought admission to the Temple of the sacred Brotherhood.

10. The council of the brotherhood convened, and Jesus stood before the hierophant. He answered all the questions that were asked with clearness and with power.

11. The hierophant exclaimed, "Rabboni of the rabbinate, why come you here? Your wisdom is the wisdom of the gods; why seek for wisdom in the halls of man?"

12. And Jesus said, "In every way of earth-life I would walk; in every hall of learning I would sit; the height that any man has gained, these I would gain;"

13. "What any man has suffered, I would meet; that I may know the griefs, the disappointments and sore temptations

of my brother man, that I may know just how to succor with those in need."

14. "I pray you brothers, let me go into your dismal crypts; I would pass the hardest of your tests."

15. The master said, "Take then the vow of secret brotherhood;" and Jesus took the vow of secret brotherhood.

16. Again the master spoke, he said, "The greatest heights are gained by those who reach the greatest depths; and you shall reach the greatest depths."

17. The guide then led the way; and in the fountain Jesus bathed. And when he had been clothed in proper garb, he stood again before the hierophant.

Chapter II

Life Works of Jesus in Joseph's Home at the Age of Seven Years

1. The home of Joseph was on Marmion Way in Nazareth. Here Mary taught her son the lessons of Elihu and Salome;

2. And Jesus greatly loved the Vedic Hymns and the Avesta; but more than all he loved to read the Psalms of David and the pungent words of Solomon.

3. The Jewish books of prophecy were his delight; and when he reached his seventh year, he needed not the books to read; for he had fixed in memory every word.

4. Joachim and his wife, grand-parents of Jesus, made a feast in honor of the child; and all their near of kin were guests.

5. And Jesus stood before the guests and said, "I had a dream, and in my dream, I stood before the sea upon a sandy beach;"

6. "The waves upon the sea were high; a storm was raging on the deep."

7. "Someone above gave me a wand. I took the wand and touched the sands, and every grain of sand became a living thing. The beach was all a mass of beauty and song."

8. "I touched the waters at my feet, and they were changed to trees, and flowers and singing birds; and everything was praising Allah."

9. "And someone spoke. I did not see the one who spoke; I heard the voice, which said, 'There is no death.'"

10. Grandmother Ann loved the child. She laid her hand on Jesus's head and said, "I saw you stand beside the sea; I saw you touch the sand; and the waves, I saw them turn to living things; and then I knew the meaning of the dream"

11. "The sea of life rolls high; the storms are great; the multitude of men are idle, listless, waiting like dead sands upon the beach."

12. "Your want is Truth; with this you touch the multitude, and every man becomes a messenger of Holy light and life."

13. "You touch the waves upon the sea of life, their turmoils cease; the very winds become a song of praise."

14. "There is no death; because the wand of Truth can change the driest bones to living things, and bring the loveliest flowers from stagnant ponds, and turn the most discordant notes to harmony and praise."

15. Joachim said, "My son, today you pass the seventh milestone of your way of life; for you are seven years of age, and we will give to you as a remembrance of this day whatever you desire. Choose that which will afford you most delight."

16. And Jesus said, "I do not want a gift, for I am satisfied. If I could make a multitude of children glad upon this day, I would be greatly pleased."

17. "Now there are many hungry boys and girls in Nazareth who would be pleased to eat with us, at this feast, and share with us the pleasures of this day."

18. "The richest gift that you can give to me is your permission to go out and find those needy ones, and bring them here that they may feast with us."

19. Joachim said, "Tis well. Go out and find the needy boys and girls, and bring them here. We will prepare enough for all."

20. And Jesus did not wait. He ran. He entered every home and hut and den of the town. He did not waste his words; he told his mission everywhere.
21. And in a little time one hundred and three score of happy children were following Jesus on Marmion way.
22. The guests made way; the banquet hall was filled with Jesus's guests; and Jesus and his mother served.
23. And there was food enough for all, and all were glad. So the birthday gift of Jesus was a crown of righteousness.

Chapter III

The Life and Works of Jesus at the Age of Ten Years

1. The great feast of Jews was on; and Joseph, Mary and their son, and many of their kin, went to Jerusalem. The child was ten years old.
2. And Jesus watched the butchers kill the lambs and birds and burn them on the altar in the name of Allah.
3. His tender heart was shocked at this display of cruelty. He asked the serving priest, "What is the purpose of this slaughter of the beasts and birds - why do you burn their flesh before Allah?"
4. The priest replied, "This is our sacrifice for sin. Allah has commanded us to do these things, and said, that in sacrifices all our sins are blotted out."
5. And Jesus said, "Will you be kind enough to tell when Allah proclaimed that sins are blotted out by sacrifices of any kind?"
6. "Did not David say that Allah requires not a sacrifice for sin? That it is sin itself to bring before His face burnt offerings for sin? Did not Isaiah say the same?"
7. The priest replied, "My child, you are beside yourself. Do you know more about the law of Allah than all of Israel? This is no place for boys to show their wit."
8. But Jesus heeded not his taunts; he went at once to Hillel and said to him,

9. "Rabboni, I would like to talk with you. I am disturbed about this service. I thought the Temple was the house of Allah; where Love and Kindness dwell."

10. "Do you not hear the bleating of those lambs; the pleading of those doves that men are killing over there? Do you not smell the awful stench of burning flesh?"

11. "Can you be kind and just, and still be filled with cruelty?"

12. "An Allah that takes delight in burning flesh and blood is not Allah of Love; he is not my Father."

13. "I want to find the Allah of Love; and, you, my master, you are wise; and surely you can tell me where to find the Allah of Love."

14. But Hillel could not give an answer to the child. His heart was stirred with sympathy. He called the child to him. He laid his hand upon his head and wept.

15. He said, "There is an Allah of Love; and you shall come with me, and, hand in hand, we will go forth and find Allah of Love."

16. And Jesus said, "Why need we go? I thought Allah was everywhere. Can we not purify our hearts and drive out cruelty and every wicked thought and make a Temple where Allah of Love can dwell?"

17. The master of the great courts felt as though he was himself a child; and that before him stood the master of all the laws.

18. He said within himself, "This child is surely a Prophet sent of Allah."

19. Then Hillel sought the parents of the child, and asked that Jesus might abide with him and learn the precepts of the law and all the lessons of the Temple.

20. His parents gave consent, and Jesus did abide in the Temple every day; and every day the master learned from Jesus many lessons of higher life.

21. And the child remained in the Temple of Hillel for a year, and then returned to his home in Nazareth. And there he wrought with Joseph as a carpenter.

Chapter IV

Jesus Talks with the Rabbi of the Ten Commands

1. Now Rabbi Barachia of Nazareth and Jesus, the son of Joseph and Mary met. The Rabbi was aid in teaching the son.

2. One morning after service in the Temple, Jesus, as he sat in silent thought, the Rabbi said to Jesus, "Which is the greatest of the ten commands?"

3. And Jesus said, "I do not see the greatest of the ten commands; I see a gold cord that runs through all the ten commands; that binds them fast and makes them one."

4. "This cord is Love; and it belongs to every word of all the ten commands."

5. "If one is full of Love, he can nothing else but worship Allah; for Allah is Love."

6. And if one is full of Love, he cannot kill; he cannot falsely testify, he cannot covet. He can do naught but honor Allah and man."

7. "If one is full of Love, he does not need commands of any kind."

8. And Rabbi Barachia said, "Your words are seasoned with the salt of wisdom that is from above. Who is the teacher who has opened up this Truth to you?"

9. And Jesus said, "I do not know any teacher opened up this Truth for me. It seems to me that Truth was never shut; that it was always opened up; for Truth is one and it is everywhere."

10. "And, if we open up the windows of our minds, the Truth will enter in and make herself at home; for Truth can find her way through any crevice, any window, any open door."

11. The Rabbi said, "What hand is strong enough to open up the windows and the doors of our minds so Truth can enter in?"

12. And Jesus said, "It seems to me that Love, the golden cord that binds the ten commands in one, is strong enough to open any human door so that Truth can enter in, and cause the heart to understand."

13. Now in the evening Jesus and his mother sat alone; and Jesus said,
14. "The Rabbi seems to think that Allah is partial in his treatments of the sons of men; that Jews are favored and blessed above all other men."
15. "I do not see how Allah can have favorites and be just."
16. "Are not the Samaritans and the Greeks and Romans just as much the children of the Holy One as are the Jews?"
17. "I think the Jews have built a wall about themselves, and they see nothing on the other side of it."
18. "They do not know that flowers are blooming over there; that sowing time belongs to anyone but the Jews."
19. "It surely would be well if we could break these barriers down so that the Jews might see that Allah has other children that are just as greatly blest"
20. "I want to go from Jewry land and meet my kin in other countries of my fatherland."

Chapter V

Jesus Again: His First Year of Divine Ministry

"The Jewish paschal feast time came. And Jesus left His mother in Capernaum, and journeyed to Jerusalem"

1. And he abode with one a Sadducee whose name was Jude.
2. And when he reached the Temple court, the multitudes were there to see the Prophet whom the people thought had come to break the yoke of Rome, and restore the kingdom of the Jews and the rules of David's throne.
3. And when the people saw him come, they said, "All hail."
4. But Jesus answered not. He saw the moneychangers in the house of Allah, and he was grieved.
5. The courts had been converted into marts of trade, and men were selling lambs and doves for the priests.
6. And Jesus called the priest and said, "Behold, for paltry gain, you have sold out the Temple of Allah!"

7. "This house ordained for prayer is now a den of thieves. Can good and evil dwell together in the courts of Allah? I tell you No!"

8. And then he drove them out and over-turned the boards.

9. He opened up the cages of the captive birds, and cut the cords that bound the lambs and set them free.

10. The priests and scribes rushed out; and would have done him harm, but the common people drove them back and stood in his defense.

11. And then the rules said, "Who is this Jesus you can call Divine?"

12. The people said, "He is the one the Prophets wrote concerning, who would come and bring the world the Love of Allah made known to men of earth, who will deliver Israel."

13. The ruler said to Jesus, "If you be the one to come, then show us a sign. Who gave you the right to drive these merchants out?"

14. And Jesus said, "There is no loyal Jew who would not give his life to save this Temple from disgrace. In this, I acted simply as a loyal Jew; and you yourselves will bear me witness to the Truth."

15. "The sign of my Messiahship will follow me in word and deed."

16. "And you may tear the Temple down; and in three days, it will be built again."

17. Now Jesus meant that they might take his life-tear down his body Temple of the Holy Breath, and he would rise again.

18. "You men of Israel, hear! This man is more than man. Take heed to what you do. I have myself heard Jesus speak, and all the winds were still."

19. "And you will see his star arise, and it will grow until it is the full orbed sun of Love."

20. And Jesus said, "Prepare, O Israel, prepare to meet your king; but you can never see the king while you press sin to your hearts."

21. "This king is Allah; the pure in heart alone can see the face of Allah and live."

Chapter VI

Jesus Presented with His Camel, Goes to Lahore Where He Abides

1. A caravan of merchantmen was journeying through the Kasmar vale as Jesus passed that way. And they were going to Lahore, a city of the land, the five-stream land.
2. The merchantmen had heard the Prophet speak; had seen his mighty works in Leh. And they were glad to see him once again.
3. And when they knew that he was going to Lahore, and then across the Sindh through Persia, and further west, and that he had no beast on which to ride.
4. They freely gave to him a noble Bactrian beast, well saddled and equipped. And Jesus journeyed with the caravan.
5. And when he reached Lahore, Ajainin and some other Brahmic priest received him with delight.
6. Ajainin was the priest who came to Jesus in the nighttime in Benares many months before and heard his words of truth.
7. And Jesus was Ajainin's guest. He taught again in many things; revealed to him the secret of the healing art.
8. He taught him how he could control the spirits of the air, the fire, the water and the earth; and explained to him the secret doctrine of forgiveness, and blotting out of sin.
9. One day Ajainin sat with Jesus in the Temple porch. A bank of wandering singers and musicians paused before the court to sing and play.
10. Their music was most rich and delicate; and Jesus said, "Among the high-bred people of the land, we have no sweeter music than these uncouth children of the wilderness bring here to us."
11. "From whence came this talent and this power? In one short life they surely could not gain such grace of voice, such knowledge of the laws of harmony and tone."
12. "These people are not young. A thousand years ago would not suffice to give them such divine expressiveness and such purity of voice and touch."

13. "Men all them prodigies. There are no prodigies. All things result from natural law."

14. "Ten thousand years ago these people mastered harmony. In days of old they trod the busy thorough-fares of life and caught the melody of birds, and played on harps of perfect form."

15. "And they have come again to learn still other lessons from the varied notes of manifests."

16. "These wandering people form a part of heaven's orchestra; and in the land of perfect things, the very angels will delight to hear them play and sing."

17. And Jesus taught the common people of Lahore. He healed their sick, and showed to them the way to rise to better things by helping others.

18. He said, "We are not rich by what we get and hold; the only things we keep are those we give away."

19. "If we would live a perfect life, give forth our life in service for our kind, and for the form of life, that men esteem the lower forms of life."

20. But Jesus could not tarry longer in Lahore. He bade the priest and other friends farewell; and then he took his camel and he went his way towards Sindh.

Chapter VII

Again Elihu's lessons - The Mysteries of Egypt

Again Elihu taught; he said, "The Indian Priests became corrupt; Brahm was forgotten in the streets; the rights of men were trampled in the dust."

1. "And then a mighty master came, a Buddha of enlightenment who turned away from wealth and all honors of the world, and found the silence in the graves and caves; and he was blest."

2. He taught the gospel of higher life, and taught men how to honor man.

3. He had no doctrine of the gods to teach; he just knew man; and so his creed was Justice, Love, and Righteousness.

4. I quote to you a few of many of the helpful words which Buddha spoke.
5. "Hate is a cruel word. If man hates you, regard it not, and you can turn the hate of men to Love, and Mercy and Good Will. Mercy is as large as all the heavens.
6. And there is good enough for all. With good destroy the bad. With generous deeds make avarice ashamed. With Truth make straight the crooked lines that errors draw; for error is but Truth distorted- gone astray.
7. And pain will follow him who speaks or acts with evil thought, as does the wheel the foot of him who draws the cart.
8. He is the greater man who conquers self than he who kills a thousand men in war.
9. He is the noble man who is himself what he believes that other men should be.
10. Return to him who does you wrong your purest love, and he will cease from doing wrong; for love will purify the heart of him who is beloved, as truly as it purifies the heart of him who loves."
11. The words of Buddha are recorded in the Indian sacred books. Attendeth them for they are part of the instructions of the Holy Breath.
12. The land of Egypt is the land of secret things.
13. The mysteries of the sages lie lock-bound in our Temples and Shrines.
14. The masters of all times and climes come here to learn. And when your sons have grown to manhood, they will finish all their studies in Egyptian schools.
15. But I have said enough. Tomorrow at the rising of the sun, we meet again.

Chapter VIII

The Council of the Seven of the World

1. In every age since time began, but seven sages lived.
2. At first of every age these sages meet to note the course of nations, people, tribes and tongues,
3. To note how far towards Justice and love the race has gone;

4. To formulate the ode of law, religious postulates and plans of rule best suited to the coming age.
5. An age had passed, and lo, another age had come. The sages must convene.
6. Now Alexandria was the center of the world's best thought; and here in Philo's home the sages met.
7. From China came Mengste; from India Vidyapati came; from Persia Kasper came; and from Assyria Ashbina came; from Greece Apollo came; Matheno was the Egyptian sage, and Philo was the chief of Hebrew thought.
8. The time was due. The council met and sat in silence seven days.
9. And the Mengste rose and said, "The wheel of time has turned once more. The race is on a higher plane of thought."
10. "The garments that our fathers wore have given out. The cherubim have woven a celestial cloth, have placed it in our hands and we must make for men new garbs."
11. "The sons of men are looking up for greater light. No longer do they care for gods hewn out of wood. They seek for Allah not made with hands."
12. "They see the beams of coming days, and yet comprehend them not."
13. "The time is ripe. And we must fashion well these garments for the race."
14. "And let us make for men new garbs of Justice, Mercy, and Love, that they may hide their nakedness when shines the light of coming days."
15. And Vidyapati said, "Our priests have all gone mad. They saw a demon in the wilds, and at him cast their lamps, and they are broken up, and not a gleam of light has any priest for men."
16. "The night is dark. The heart of India calls for light."
17. "The priesthood cannot be reformed; it is already dead; its greatest needs are graves and funeral chants."
18. "The new age calls for liberty - the kind that makes each man a priest; enables him to go alone and lay his offerings on the Shrine of Allah."

19. And Kaspar said, “In Persia people walk in fear. They do the good for fear to do the wrong.”
20. “The devil is the greatest power in our land. And, though a myth, he dandles on his knees both youth and age.”
21. “Our land is dark; and evil prospers in the dark.”
22. “Fear rides on every passing breeze, and lurks in every form of life.”
23. “The fear of evil is a myth; is an illusion and snare; but it will live until some mighty power shall come to raise the ethers to the plane of light.”
24. “When this shall come to pass, the Magian land will glory in the light. The soul of Persia calls for Light.”

Chapter IX

Opening Address of Jesus with the Seven Sages - Seven Days Silence

1. Ashbina said, “Assyria is the land of doubt. The chariot of my people that in which they mostly ride is labeled, ‘DOUBT’”.
2. “Once Faith walked in Babylon and she was bright and fair; but she was clothed in such white robes that men became afraid of her.”
3. “And every wheel began to turn; and Doubt made war on her and drove her from the land, and she came back no more.”
4. “In form man worships Allah, the one; in heart they are not sure that Allah exists.”
5. “Faith worships at the Temple of one not seen; but Doubt must see her god.”
6. “The greatest need of all Assyria is faith; a faith that seasons everything that is with certainty.”
7. And then Apollo said, “The greatest needs of Greece are true conceptions of Allah the one.”
8. “In Greece, it is rudderless for every thought may be a god to worship as Allah.
9. “The plane of thought is broad, and full of sharp antagonists. And so the circle of the gods is filled with enmity, with wars and base intrigues.”

10. "Greece needs a master-mind to stand above the gods; to raise the mind of men away from many gods to Allah the one."
11. "We know the light is coming over the hills-Allah speed the light."
12. Matheno said, "Behold this land of Egypt of the dead."
13. "Our Temples long have been the tombs of hidden things of time. Our Temple crypts and caves are dark."
14. "In light there is no secret thing. The sun reveals all hidden truth. There are no mysteries in Allah."
15. Behold the rising sun. His beams are entering every door; yes; every crevice of the mystic crypts of Mizraim."
16. "We hail the light. All Egypt craves the light."
17. And Philo said, "The need of Hebrew thought and life is Liberty."
18. "The Hebrew Prophets, seers and givers of the law were men of power, men of holy thought; and they bequeathed to us a system of love that was ideal; one strong enough to lead our people to the goal of perfectness."
19. "But carnal minds repudiated this law of love, and filled the minds with selfishness. And purity in heart became a myth. The people were enslaved."
20. "But when he comes who is to come, he will proclaim emancipation for the slaves. My people will be free."
21. "Behold, for Allah has made incarnate, wisdom, love and light which he called, Immanuel."
22. "To him is given the key to open up the dawn. And here, as man, he walked with us."
23. And then the council chamber door was opened; and the Logos stood among the sages of the world."
24. Again the sages sat in silence seven days.

Chapter X

Meeting of the Seven Sages to Make Laws for the Coming Age for the Nations of the Earth.

Now when the sages were refreshed, they opened up the book of life and read.

1. They read the story of the life of man; of all his struggles, losses and gains, and in the light of past events and deeds, they saw what would be best for him in coming years.
2. They knew the kind of law and precepts suited to his estate. They saw the highest Allah-Ideal that the race could comprehend.
3. Upon the seven postulates these sages were to formulate the law of life of the coming age that souls may rest.
4. Now Mengste was the oldest sage. He took the chair of chief, and said,
5. "Man is not far enough advanced to live by faith. He cannot comprehend the things his eyes see not."
6. "He yet is child; and during all the coming age must be taught by pictures, symbols, rites and forms."
7. "His God must be a human God. He cannot see Allah by faith."
8. "And he cannot rule himself. The king must rule, the man must serve."
9. "The age that follows this will be the age of man- the age of faith."
10. In that blest age the human race will see without the aid of carnal eyes; will hear the soundless sound, will know the Spirit-Allah."
11. "The age we enter is the preparation age; and all the schools must be designed in a simple way that men may comprehend."
12. "And man cannot originate. He builds by patterns that he can see. So, in this council, we must carve out patterns for the coming age."
13. "And we must formulate the gnosis of the empire of the soul which rests on seven."

14. "Each sage, in turn, shall form a postulate; and these shall be the basis of the creeds of men until the perfect age shall come."

15. Then Mengste wrote the first.

16. "All things are thought; all life is thought-activity. The multitudes of beings are but phases of the one great thought made manifest. Lo, Allah is thought, and thought is Allah."

17. Then Vidyapati wrote the second postulate.

18. "Eternal thought is one. In essence it is two - intelligence and force; and, when they breathe a child is born; this child is Love."

19. "And thus the Triune Allah stands forth, whom men call father, mother, son."

20. "This Triune Allah is one; but like the one of light, in essence he is seven."

21. "And when the Triune Allah breathes forth, lo, seven spirits stand before his face. These are Creative attributes."

22. "Men call them lesser gods, and in their image they made man."

23. And Kaspar wrote the third.

24. "Man was a thought of Allah formed in the image of the Septonate, clothed in the substance of soul."

25. "And his desires were strong. He sought to manifest on every plane of life. And for himself he made a body of the ethers of the earthy forms; and so he descended to the plane of earth."

26. "In this descent he lost his birth-right, lost his harmony with Allah, made discordant all the notes of life."

27. "Inharmony and evil are the same. So evil is the hand-work of man."

28. Ashbina wrote the fourth.

29. "Seeds do not germinate in light. They do not grow until they find the soil and hide themselves away from light."

30. "Man was evolved a seed of everlasting life; but in the ethers of the Triune Allah, the light was far too great for seeds to grow."

31. "And so man sought the soil of carnal life; and in the darksomeness of earth he found a place where he could germinate and grow."
32. "The seed has taken root and grown full well."
33. "The tree of life is rising from the soil of earthy things, and, under natural law, is reaching up to perfect form."
34. "There are no supernatural acts of Allah to lift a man from carnal life to spirit blessedness. He grows as grows the plant; and, in due time is perfected."
35. "The quality of soul that makes it possible for man to rise to spirit life is purity."

Chapter XI

Jesus Reveals the Marriage Law of Man and Wife from Allah

1. The law forbids adultery; but, in the eyes of the law, adultery is an overt act; the satisfaction of the sensuous self, outside the marriage bonds.
2. Now, marriage, in the sight of the law, is but a promise made by man and woman, by the sanction of the priest, to live together until death.
3. No priest or officer has the power from Allah to bind two souls in wedded Love.
4. What is a marriage tie? It is not what the priest may say or do. There is but one true marriage; and Allah alone can perform this marriage.
5. It is the love of Allah that finds its way into the two - man and woman's hearts; and that is all ever to be. Your priests cannot cause this to be.
6. It is the promise of the two that they will love each other until death.
7. Is love a passion that is subject to the will of man?
8. Can man pick up his love as he would a gem, and lay it down or give it out to anyone?
9. Can love be bought and sold like sheep?

10. Love is the power of Allah that binds two souls and makes them one. There is no power on earth that can dissolve this bond.
11. The bodies may be forced apart by man or death for just a little time, but they will meet again.
12. Now, in this bond of Allah, we find the marriage tie. All other unions are but bonds of straw; and they who live in them commit adultery.
13. But more than this; the man or woman who indulges lustful thoughts commits adultery.
14. Whom Allah has joined together, man cannot part. Whom man has joined together lie in sin.
15. But lo, I say that he who in the heart desires to possess that which is not his own, is a thief in the sight of Allah. The things which men see not with eyes of flesh are of more worth than the thing that men can see.
16. A good name is worth a thousand times a mine of gold; and he who says a word, or does a deed that injures or defames that name is a thief.
17. Upon the table of the law we read, "Thou shalt not covet anything."
18. To covet is an all-consuming wish to have anything that is not right for anyone to have; and such wish in the spirit of the law is theft.

Chapter XII

Jesus Explains to Kaspar the Meaning of Silence and the Wisdom of Allah in Man

1. Now, in the early morning Jesus came again to teach and heal. A light not comprehended shown about as though some mighty spirit overshadowed him.
2. A Magnus noted this and asked him privately to tell from whence his wisdom came, and what is the meaning of the light.
3. And Jesus said, "There is a silence where the soul may meet its God-Allah; and there the fount of wisdom is; and all who

enter are immersed in light and filled with wisdom, love and power."

4. The Magnus said, "Tell me about this silence and this light that I may go and there abide."

5. And Jesus said, "The silence is not circumscribed; it is not a place closed in with walls or rocky steeps, nor guarded by the swords of man."

6. "Men carry with them all the time the secret place where they meet Allah."

7. "It matters not where men abide; on mountaintop, in the deep vale, in the marts of trade or in a quiet home, they may at one time fling wide the door of the soul and find the house of Allah. It is within the soul."

8. "One may not be so much disturbed by noise of business and words and thoughts of men it goes all alone into the valley or the mountain pass."

9. "And when life's heavy load is pressing hard, it is far better to go out and seek a quiet place to pray and meditate."

10. "The silence is the kingdom of the soul, which is not seen by human eyes."

11. "When in silence, phantom forms may flit before the mind; but they are all subservient to the will. The master soul may speak, and they are gone."

12. "If you would find this silence of the soul, you must yourself prepare the way. None but the pure in heart may enter here."

13. "And you must lay aside all fears and doubts and troubled thoughts."

14. "Your human will must be absorbed by love divine; then you will come into a consciousness of the Holy Breath."

15. "You are within a holy place, and you will see upon a living shrine the candle of Allah aflame."

16. "And when you see it burning there, look deep within the Temple of your brain; you will see it all aglow."

17. "In every part from head to foot are candles all in place, just waiting to be lighted by the flaming torch of Love."

18. "And when you see the candles all aflame, just look and you will see, with eyes of soul, the waters of the fount of wisdom rushing on; and you may drink and there abide."
19. "And the curtains part; and you are where the Ark of Allah rests, whose covering is the mercy seat."
20. "Fear not to lift the sacred board; the tables of the law are in the Ark concealed."
21. "Take them and read them well; for they contain all the precepts that man will ever need."
22. "And in the Ark the magic wand, for they contain all prophecy, lies waiting for our hands. It is the key to all the hidden meanings of present, future and past."
23. "The Cherubim have guarded well for every soul this treasure box; and whosoever will may enter in and find his own."
24. Now Kaspar heard the Hebrew master speak and he exclaimed, "Behold, the wisdom of Allah has come to men."
25. And Jesus went his way, and in the sacred grove of Cyrus was met. He taught and healed the sick.

Chapter XIII

Jesus's Holy Answer to Lamaas

1. Now, after they had dined, the guests and Jesus all were in a spacious hall in Mary's home.
2. And Lamaas said, "Pray tell us, Jesus, is this the dawn of peace?"
3. "Have we come forth unto the time when men will war no more?"
4. "Are you indeed the prince of peace that holy men have said would come?"
5. And Jesus said, "Peace reigns today; it is the peace of death."
6. "A stagnant pool abides in peace. When waters cease to move they soon are laden with the seeds of death. Corruption dwells in every drop."
7. "The living waters always leap and skip about like lambs in spring."

8. "The nations are corrupt. They sleep within the arms of death, and they must be aroused before it is too late."

9. "In life we find antagonists at work. Allah sent me here to stir unto its depths the waters of the sea of life."

10. "Peace follows strife. I come to slay this peace of earth. The prince of peace must first be prince of strife."

11. "This leaven of truth which I have brought to men will stir the demons up, and nations, cities, families will be at peace with themselves."

12. "The five that have been dwelling in a home in peace will be divided not; and two shall war against three."

13. "The son will stand against his sire; the mother and daughter will contend. Yea; strife will reign in every home."

14. "Then self and greed and doubt will rage into a fever heat. And then, because of me, the earth will be baptized in human blood."

15. "But right is king; and when the smoke is cleared away, the nations will learn war no more. The prince of peace will come to reign.

16. "Behold, the signs of what I say are in the sky but men can see them not."

17. "When men behold a cloud rise in the west they say a shower of rain will come; and so it does. And when the wind blows from the south, they say the weather will be hot; and it is so"

18. "Lo, men can read the signs of earth and sky, but they cannot discern the signs of the Holy Breath; but you shall know."

19. "The storms of wrath come on. The carnal man will seek a cause to hale you into court, and cast you into prison cells."

20. "And, when these times shall come, let wisdom guide; do not resent. Resentment makes more strong the wrath of evil men."

21. "There is a little sense of Justice and of Mercy in the vilest men of earth."

22. "By taking heed to what you do and say, and trusting in the guidance of the Holy Breath, you may inspire this sense to grow."

23. "You thus may make the wrath of men to praise Allah."
24. And Jesus went his way and came unto Bethsada and taught.

Chapter XIV

Jesus Receives the Mystic Name and Number and Passed the First Brother-hood Test

The master took down from the wall a scroll on which was written down the number and name of every attribute, character; and he said.

1. "The cCrcle is the symbol of the perfect man; and the Seven is the number of the perfect man."
2. "The Logos is the perfect word; that which creates, that which destroys, and that which saves."
3. "This Hebrew master is the Logos of the Holy One, the Circle of the human race, the Seven of the time."
4. And in the record book, the scribe wrote down, "The Logos, Circle, Seven," and thus was Jesus known.
5. The master said, "The Logos will give heed to what I say. No man can enter into light till he has found himself; go forth and search till you have found your soul and then return."
6. The guide led Jesus to a room in which the light was faint and mellow like the light of early dawn.
7. The chamber walls were marked with mystic signs, with hieroglyphs and sacred texts; and in the chamber Jesus found himself alone where he remained for many days.
8. He read the sacred texts, thought out the meanings of the hieroglyphs and sought the import of the master's charge to find himself.
9. A revelation came. He got acquainted with his soul. He found himself; then he was not alone.
10. One night he slept, and at midnight hour a door that he had not observed was opened and a priest in somber garb came in and said,
11. "My brother, pardon me for coming in at this unseemly hour; but I have come to save your life."

12. "You are the victim of a cruel plot. The priests of Heliopolis are jealous of your fame, and they have said that you will never leave these gloomy crypts alive."

13. "The higher priests do not go forth to teach the world; and you are doomed to Temple servitude."

14. "Now, if you would be free, you must deceive these priests; must tell them you are here to stay for life."

15. "And then you will have gained all that you wish to gain, I will return; and, by a secret way, will lead you forth that you may go in peace."

16. And Jesus said, "My brother man, would you come here to teach deceit? Am I within these holy walls to learn the wiles of vile hypocrisy?"

17. "Nay, man; my father scorns deceit; and I am here to do Hi will."

18. "Deceive these priests? Not while the sun shines! What I have said I have said. I will be true to them, to Allah and to myself."

19. And then the tempter left, and Jesus was again alone; but in a little time a white -robed priest appeared and said,

20. "Well done. The Logos has prevailed. This is the trial chamber of hypocrisy." And then he led the way, and Jesus stood before the judgment seat.

21. And all the brothers stood. The hierophant came forth and laid hands on Jesus's head and placed within his hand a scroll on which was written just one word; "SINCERITY". And not a word was said.

22. The guide again appeared and led the way, in the spacious room replete with everything a student craves, was Jesus bade to rest and wait.

Chapter XV

Jesus Passes the Second Brother-hood Test - Justice

The Logos did not care to rest. He said, "Why wait in this luxurious room? I need not rest; my father's work upon me presses hard."

1. "I would go on and learn my lessons all. If there are trials, let them come; for every victory over self gives added strength."

2. And then the guide led on. And in a chamber dark as night was Jesus placed and left alone. And days were spent in this deep solitude.

3. And Jesus slept; and in the dead of the night, a secret door was opened, and in priest's attire two men came in, each carrying in his hand a little flickering lamp.

4. Approaching Jesus, one spoke out and said, "Young man, our hearts are grieved because of what you suffer in these fearful dens, and we have come as friends to bring you light and show the way to liberty."

5. "We, once like you were in these dens confined, and thought that through these weird, uncanny ways we could attain to blessedness and power;"

6. "But, in a luckful moment, we were undeceived, and making use of all our strength, we broke our chains; and then we learned that all this service is corruption in disguise. These priests are criminals just hid away."

7. "They boast of sacrificial rites; they offer to their gods, and burn them while alive, poor birds and beasts; yea children, women and men."

8. And now they keep you here; and at a certain time, may offer you in sacrifice.

9. We pray you brother, break your chains. Come go with us; accept of freedom while you may."

10. And Jesus said. "Your little tapers show the light you bring. Pray, who are you? The words of man are worth no more than is the man himself."

11. "These Temple walls are strong and high; how gained you entrance to this place?"

12. The men replied, "Beneath these walls are hidden ways and we who have been priests spent months and years within these dens and know all of them"

13. "Then you are traitors!" Jesus said; "A traitor is a friend who betrays another man, is never a man to trust."

14. "If one has only reached the plane of treachery, he is a lover of deceit, and will betray a friend to save his selfish self."

15. "Behold, you men, or whatsoever you be, your words fall lightly on my ears."

16. "Could I prejudge these hundred priests, turn traitor to myself and them, because of what you say, when you confess your treachery?"

17. "No man can judge for me; and if I judge before testimony all is in, I might not judge aright."

18. "Nay, men; by whatsoever way you came, return. My soul prefers the darkness of the grave to little flickering light like these you bring."

19. "My conscience rules. What these, my brothers have to say, I will hear; and, when the testimony all is in, I will decide. You cannot judge for me, nor I for you."

20. "Be gone! You men, be gone! And leave to me this charming light; for, while the sun shines not, within my soul there is a light surpassing that of sun and moon!"

21. Then, with an angry threat that they would do him harm, the vile tempters left; and Jesus was alone.

22. Again the white-robed priest appeared and led the way; and Jesus stood again before the hierophant.

23. And not a word was said; but in his hands the master placed as scroll on which the word "JUSTICE" was inscribed.

24. And Jesus was the master of the phantom forms of prejudice and of treachery.

Chapter XVI

Jesus Passes the Third Brother-hood Test - FAITH

The Logos waited seven days; and then was taken to the Hall of Fame, a chamber rich in furnishings, and lighted up with gold and silver lamps.

1. The colors of its ceiling decorations, furnishing and walls were blue and gold.

2. Its shelves were filled with books of masterminds. The paintings and the statues were the works of highest art.

3. And Jesus was entranced with all this elegance and these manifests of thought. He read the sacred books, and sought the meaning of the symbols and the hieroglyphs.

4. And when he was absorbed in deepest thought, a priest approached and said,

5. "Behold the glory of this place! My brother you are blest. Few men of earth so young have reached such heights of fame."

6. "Now, if you do not waste your life in search for hidden things that man can never comprehend, you may be founder of a school of thought that will assure you endless fame."

7. For your philosophy is deeper far than that of Plato; and your teachings please the common people more than those of Socrates.

8. Why seek for mystic light within these antiquated dens? Go forth and walk with men, and they will honor you.

9. And, after all, these weird initiations may be myths; and your messiah hopes but illusions of the hour.

10. I would advise you to renounce uncertain things, and choose the course that leads to certain fame.

11. And thus, the priest - a demon in disguise - sang siren songs of unbelief. And Jesus meditated long and well on what he said.

12. The conflict was a bitter one; for king ambition is a sturdy foe to fight.

13. For forty days the higher self wrestled with the lower self. And then the fight was on.

14. FAITH rose triumphant; unbelief was not; ambition covered up his face and fled away. And Jesus said,
15. "The wealth, the honor and the fame of earth are but the baubles of the hour."
16. "When this short span of earthly life has been measured out, man's bursting baubles will be buried with his bones."
17. "Yes; what man does for his selfish self will make no markings on the credit side of life."
18. "The good that man for other men shall do, becomes a ladder strong, on which the soul may climb to wealth and power and fame of Allah's own kind that cannot pass away."
19. "Give me the poverty of men; the consciousness of duty done in love; the approbation of Allah, and I will be content."
20. And he lifted up his eyes to heaven, and said,
21. "My Father Allah, I thank thee for this hour. I ask not for the glory of myself; I fain would be a keeper of the Temple gates, and serve my brother-man."
22. Again was Jesus called to stand before the hierophant. Again no word was said; but in his hands the master placed a scroll on which was written, "FAITH".
23. And Jesus bowed his head in humble thanks and went his way.

Chapter XVII

Jesus Passes the Fourth Brother-hood Test; Takes the Fourth Degree of Adept

Whether other certain days had passed, the guide led Jesus to the hall of mirth; a hall most richly furnished, and replace with everything a carnal heart could wish.

1. The choicest viands and most delicious wines were on the boards. And maids in gay attire served all with grace and cheerfulness.
2. And men and women richly clad were there. And they were wild with joy. They sipped from cheery cups of mirth.

3. And Jesus watched the happy throng in silence for a time; and then a man in garb of sage came up and said, "Most happy is the man who, like the bee, can gather sweets from every flower."

4. "The wise man is the one who seeks for pleasure, and can find it everywhere."

5. "At best, man's life on earth is short. And then he dies and goes he knows not where."

6. "Then let us eat and drink and dance and sing; let us get joy of life, for death comes apace."

7. "It is but foolishness to spend a life for other men. Behold, I die and lie together in the grave where none can know, and none can show forth gratitude."

8. But Jesus answered not. Upon the tinseled guests, in all their rounds of mirth, he gazed in silent thought.

9. And then among the guests, he saw a man whose clothes were coarse, who showed in face and hand, the lines of toil and want.

10. The giddy throng found pleasure in abusing him. They jostled him against the walls and laughed at this discomfiture.

11. And a poor frail woman came, who carried in her face and form, the marks of sin and shame. And, without mercy, she was spit upon.

12. And a little child, with timid ways and hungry men came in and asked for just a morsel of their food.

13. But she was driven out uncared for and unloved; and still the merry dance went on.

14. And when the pleasure-seekers urged that Jesus join them in their mirth, he said,

15. "How could I seek for pleasure for myself while others are in want? How can I think that, while the children cry for bread, while those in haunts of sin call out for sympathy and love, that I can fill myself too full with the good things of life?"

16. "I tell you, nay! We all are kin, each one a part of the great human heart."

17. "I cannot see myself apart from that poor man who you so scorned and crowded to the wall."

18. "Nor from the one in female garb, who came up from the haunts of vice to ask for sympathy and love; and who, by you, was so ruthlessly pushed back into her den of sin."

19. "Nor from that little child you drive from your midst to suffer in the cold, bleak winds of night."

20. "I tell you, men; what you have done to them, my kindred, you have done to me."

21. "You have insulted me in your own home. I cannot stay. I will go forth and find that child, that woman and that man, and give them help until my life's blood all has ebbed away."

22. "I will call it pleasure when I help the helpless, feed the hungry, clothe the naked, heal the sick, and speak good words of cheer to those unloved, discouraged, and depressed."

23. "And this that you call mirth is but a phantom of the night; but flashes of the fire of passion painting pictures on the walls of time."

24. And while the Logos spoke the white-robed priest came in and said to him. "The council waits for you."

25. Then, Jesus stood again before the bar. Again no word was said. The hierophant placed in his hand a scroll on which was written, "PHILANTHROPY".

26. And Jesus was a victor over selfish self.

Chapter XVIII

Jesus Passes the Fifth Adept Degree - Heroism

1. The sacred Temple groves were rich in statues, monuments and shrines; here Jesus loved to walk and meditate.

2. And after he had conquered self, he talked with nature in these groves for forty days.

3. And then the guide took chains and bound him hand and foot, and cast him into a den of hungry beasts, of unclean birds and creeping things.

4. The den was dark as night. The wild beasts howled; the birds, in fury, screamed, the reptiles hissed.

5. And Jesus said, "Who is it that did bind me thus? Why did I meekly sit to be bound down with chains?"

6. "I tell you, none has power to bind the human soul. Of what are fetters made?"

7. And in his might, he rose; and what he thought were chains were only worthless cords, that parted at his touch.

8. And then he laughed and said, "The chains that bind men to the carcasses of earth are forged in fancy's shop; are made of air and welded in illusion's fires."

9. "If man will stand and use the power of will, his chains will fall like worthless rags; for will and faith are stronger than the stoutest chains that men have ever made."

10. And Jesus stood erect among the hungry beasts and birds and said, "What is this darkness that envelopes me?"

11. "'Tis but the absence of the light. And what is light? 'Tis but the breath of Allah vibrating in the rhythm of rapid thought."

12. And then he said, "Let there be light!" And, with a mighty will, he stirred the ethers up, and their vibrations reached the plane of light; and there was light.

13. The darkness of that den of night became the brightness of a new-born day.

14. And then he looked to see the beasts and birds and creeping things. Lo, they were not.

15. And Jesus said, "Of what is soul afraid? Fear is the chariot in which man rides to death!"

16. "And when he finds himself within the chamber of the dead, he learns that he has been deceived; his chariot was a myth, and death a fancy child."

17. "But some day all men's lessons will be learned. And from the den of unclean beasts and birds and creeping things, he will rise to walk in light."

18. And Jesus saw a ladder made of gold, on which he climbed; and at the top the white-robed priest awaited him.

19. Again he stood before the council bar. Again no word was said. Again the hierophant reached for his hand to bless.

20. He placed in Jesus's hand another scroll. And on this one was written "HEROISM".

21. The Logos had encountered fear and all his phantom hosts; and, in the conflict, he achieved the victory.

Chapter XIX

Jesus Takes the Sixth Degree and Passed the Sixth Adept Chamber of the Eastern Sages.

In all the land there was no place more grandly furnished than the beauty parlors of the Temple of the Sun.

1. Few students ever entered these rooms. The priests guarded them with awe, and called them halls of mysteries.

2. When Jesus had attained the victory over fear, he gained the right to enter here.

3. The guide led on the way. And, after passing many richly furnished rooms, they reached the hall of harmony, and there was Jesus left alone.

4. Among the instruments of music was a harpsichord. And Jesus sat in thoughtful mood, inspecting it, when quietly a maiden of entrancing beauty came into the hall.

5. She did not seem to notice Jesus as he sat and mused so busy with his thoughts.

6. She found her place beside the harpsichord. She touched the chords most gently, and she sang the songs of Israel.

7. And Jesus was entranced; such beauty he had never seen, such music he had never heard.

8. The maiden sang her songs. She didn't seem to know that any one was near. She went her way.

9. And Jesus, talking with himself, said out, "What is the meaning of this incident? I did not know that such entrancing beauty and such queen-like loveliness were ever found among the sons of men."

10. "I did not know that voice of angel ever graced a human form; or that seraphic music ever came from human lips."

11. For days he sat entranced. The current of his thoughts was changed. He thought of nothing but the singer and her songs.

12. He longed to see her once again and, after days, she came. She spoke and laid her hand upon his head.

13. Her touch thrilled all his soul; and, for a time, he forgot the work that he was sent to do.

14. Few were the words the maiden said. She went her way; but then the heart of Jesus had been touched.

15. A love-flame had been kindled in his soul, and he was brought to face the sorest trial of life.

16. He could not sleep, nor could he eat. The thoughts of the maiden came; they would not go. His carnal nature called aloud for her companionship.

17. And then, he said, "Lo, I have conquered every foe that I have met, and shall I now be conquered by carnal love?"

18. "My Father sent me her to show the power of love-divine; that love that reaches every living thing."

19. "Shall this pure universal love be all absorbed by carnal love? Shall I forget all creatures else, and lose my life in this fair maiden? Though she is the highest type of beauty, purity and love."

20. Into its very depths, his soul was stirred; and long he wrestled with this angel-idol of his heart.

21. But when the day was almost lost his higher-ego rose in might. He found himself again, and then he said,

22. "Although my heart shall break, I will not fail in this my hardest task. I will be victor over carnal love."

23. And when again the maiden came and offered him her hand and heart, he said,

24. "Fair one, your very presence thrills me with delight. Your voice is benediction to my soul. My human self would fly with you, and be contented in your love."

25. "But all the world is craving for a love that I have come to manifest."

26. "I must then, bid you go, but we will meet again. Our ways on earth will not be cast apart."

27. "I see you in the hurrying throngs of earth as minister of love. I hear your voice in song that wins the hearts of men to better things."

28. And then in sorry and in tears the maiden went away; and Jesus was alone again.

29. Instantly the great bells of the Temple rang. The grotto blazed with light.

30. The hierophant himself appeared, and said, "All hail triumphant Logos; Hail the conqueror of carnal love stands on the height."

31. And then he placed in Jesus's hand a scroll on which was written, "LOVE DIVINE"

32. Together they passed from the grotto of the beautiful Temple, and in the banquet hall a feast was served, and Jesus was the honored guest.

Chapter XX

The Adept Chamber of the Dead. The Mysteries of Egypt.

The senior course of study now was opened up. And Jesus entered and became a pupil of the hierophant.

1. He learned the secrets of the mystic lore of Egyptland, the mysteries of life and death and of the world beyond the circle of the sun.

2. When he had finished all the studies of the senior course, he went into the chamber of the dead that he might learn the ancient methods of preserving from decay, the bodies of the dead, and here he wrought.

3. And carriers brought the body of a widow's son to be embalmed. The weeping mother followed close. Her grief was great.

4. And Jesus said, "Good woman, dry your tears. You follow but an empty house. Your son is in it not."

5. "You weep because your son is dead. Death is not a cruel word. Your son can never die."

6. "He had a task assigned to do in garb of flesh. He came; he did his work; and then he laid the flesh aside; he did not need it more."

7. "Beyond the human sight, he has another work to do, and he will do it well and then pass to other tasks. And by and by he will attain the crown of perfect life."

8. "And what your son has done, and what he yet must do, we all must do."

9. "Now, if you harbor grief and give your sorrows vent, they will grow greater every day. They will absorb your very life until at last you will be naught, we down with bitter tears."

10. "Instead of helping him, you grieve your son by your deep grief. He seeks your solace now as he has ever done; is glad when you are glad, is saddened when you grieve."

11. "Go bury deep your woes, and smile at grief; and lose yourself in helping others dry their tears."

12. "With duty done comes happiness and joy. And gladness cheers the hearts of those who have passed on."

13. The weeping woman turned and went her way to find happiness in helpfulness; to bury deep her sorrows in a ministry of joy.

14. Then other carriers came and brought the body of a mother to the chamber of the dead. And just one mourner followed, she, a girl of tender years.

15. And as the cortege neared the door, the child observed a wounded bird in sore distress. A cruel hunter's dart had pierced its breast.

16. And she left following the dead, and went to help the living bird.

17. With tenderness and love she folded to her breast the wounded bird, then hurried to her place.

18. And Jesus said to her, "Why did you leave your dead to save a wounded bird?"

19. The maiden said, "This lifeless body needs no help from me. My mother taught me this."

20. "My mother taught that grief and selfish love and hopes and fears are but reflexes from the lower self."

21. "That what we sense is but small waves upon the rolling billows of a life."

22. "These all will pass away. They are unreal."

23. "Tears flow from hearts of flesh. The spirit never weeps; and I am longing of the day when I can walk in the light where tears are wiped away."

24. "My mother taught that all emotions are sprays that rise from human love and hope and fears; that perfect bliss cannot be ours till we have conquered these."

25. And in the presence of that child did Jesus bow his head in reverence. He said,

26. "For days and months and years I have sought to learn this highest truth that man can learn on earth; and here a child, fresh brought to earth, has told it all in one short breath."

27. No wonder David said, Oh Allah, our Lord; how excellent is thy name in all the earth!"

28. "Out of the mouth of babes and sucklings hast thou ordained strength."

29. And then he laid his hand upon the maiden's head and said, "I am sure the blessings of my Father Allah will rest upon you, Child, forever."

Chapter XXI

Jesus, The Prophet Had Finished His Tasks, and Must Now Go to the Sons of Men with Love Divine and Peace on Earth

The work of Jesus was done; and now he must go to teach the sons of men. And in the Temple he stood and said, "The son of man has come to bring the light - the light of life."

1. And all the brothers stood and said, "This is a royal day for all the hosts of the earth; for salvation has come to all the children of men. Six times before the bar, six times a conqueror."

2. And then one said to Jesus, "Brother-man, most excellent of men, in all the Temple tests you have won out."

3. "Upon your brow I place this diadem; and in the great assembly of all the world and heaven, you are the mastermind of all."

4. "Now man can do no more; but Allah himself will speak and confirm your title. Go your way and teach peace on earth, good will to man."

5. And while the hierophant yet spoke the Temple bells rang out in love; and the Logos journeyed on his way, a conqueror.

Chapter XXII

Jesus Addresses the Seven Sages - Goes to Galilee

1. The seven days of silence passed. And Jesus, sitting with the sages said,

2. "The history of life is well condensed in these immortal postulates. These are the seven hills on which the Holy City shall be built. These are the seven sure foundation stones on which the Temple shall stand."

3. "In taking up the work assigned for me to do, I am full conscious of the perils of the way. The cup will be a bitter one to drink; and human nature well might shrink."

4. "But I have lost my will in that of Holy Breath. And so I go my way to speak and act as I am moved to speak and act by the Holy Breath."

5. "The words I speak are not my own; they are the words of Him whose will I do."

6. "Man is not far enough advanced in sacred thought to comprehend within the Temple of Allah; so the work that Allah gave me to do is to teach men to build the Temple of Love within."

7. "I am sent to be a pattern of the Temple that man must build within."

8. "My task as builder lies within my native land. And there upon was the Temple of might Allah made known - the Allah in man."

9. "And from the lower estate of men, I will select seven men who will represent the Temple of Love - Allah in man."

10. "The house of Judah, my own kindred in flesh, will comprehend but little of my mission to the world;"

11. "And they will spurn me, scorn my work, accuse me falsely, bid me, take me to the judgment seat of carnal men who will convict and slay me."
12. "But man can never slay the truth. Though banished it will come again, in greater power; for truth will subjugate the world."
13. "The Temple will live, though carnal men will prostitute its sacred laws, symbolic rites and forms for selfish ends; and make it but outward show. The few will find through it the kingdom of the soul."
14. "And when the better age shall come, the Temple will stand upon the seven postulates, and will be built according to the pattern given."
15. "The time has come. I go my way unto the world; and, by the power of living faith, and by the strength that you give me."
16. "And in the name of our God-Allah, the kingdom of soul shall be established and seven hills." And all the sages said, "Amen", and Jesus went his way.

Chapter XXIII

Jesus Received the News of His Father's Death. Writes a Letter to His Mother

One day as Jesus stood beside the Ganges busy with his work; a caravan returning from the west drew near.

1. And one approaching Jesus said, "We come to you just from your native land, and bring you welcome news."
2. Your father is no more on earth; your mother grieves; and none can comfort her. She wonders whether you are still alive or not. She longs to see you once again."
3. And Jesus bowed his head in silent thought. And then he wrote; of what he wrote, this is the sum:
4. "My mother, noblest of woman kind, a man just from my native land has brought me word."
5. "My mother, all is well. Is well for father, is well for you."
6. "His work in this earth-round is done; and it is nobly done."

7. "In all the walks of life, men cannot charge him with deceit, dishonesty, nor wrong intent."

8. "Here in this round, he finished man heavy tasks; and he has gone hence, prepared to solve the problems of the round of soul."

9. "Our Father Allah is with him there as he was with him here. And there his angel guards his footsteps, lest he goes astray."

10. "Why should you weep? Tears cannot conquer grief. There is no power in grief to mend a broken heart."

11. "The plane of grief is idleness. The busy soul can never grieve; it has no time for grief."

12. "When grief comes trooping through the heart, just lose yourself, and plunge deep into the ministry of love, and grief is not."

13. "Yours is a ministry of love; and all the world is calling out for love."

14. "Then let the past go with the past. Rise from cares of carnal things and give your life for those who live."

15. "And if you lose your life in serving life, you will be sure to find it in the morning sun, the evening dew, in songs of birds, in flowers and in the stars of night."

16. "In just a little while our problems of earth-round will be solved; and, when your sums are all worked, it will be pleasure unalloyed for you to enter wider fields of usefulness, to solve the greater problems of the soul."

17. "Strive, then, to be content; and I will come to you some day and bring you richer gifts of gold or precious stones."

18. "I am sure that John will care for you; supplying all your needs. And I am with you always."

Signed,

Jehoshua

19. And by the hands of one, a merchant going to Jerusalem, he sent this letter on its way.

III. Koran Questions for Moorish Americans

101s and Additional Laws

Source:

Noble Drew Ali, Prophet, "Koran Questions for Moorish Americans: 101s and Additional Laws," in *"I'm Going to Repeat Myself": A Compilation of Artifacts Authored by Noble Prophet Drew Ali & The M.S.T. of A.*, edited by Sis. Tauheedah S. Najee-Ullah El, 14-22. Redondo Beach, CA: Califa Media, 2014.

Moorish American Prayer

ALLAH, the Father of the Universe, the Father of Love, Truth, Freedom and Justice. ALLAH is my protector, my guide, and my Salvation by night and by day, through his Holy Prophet DREW ALI [Amen].

---

1. Who made you? ALLAH.
2. Who is ALLAH? ALLAH is the father of the Universe.
3. Can we see Him? No.
4. Where is the nearest place we can meet Him? In the heart.
5. Who is Noble Drew Ali? He is ALLAH'S Prophet.
6. What is a Prophet? A Prophet is a thought of Allah manifested in flesh.
7. What is the duty of a Prophet? To save nations from the wrath of ALLAH.
8. Who is the founder of the MOORISH SCIENCE TEMPLE OF AMERICA? Nobel Drew Ali.
9. What year was the MOORISH SCIENCE TEMPLE OF AMERICA founded? 1913 A.D.
10. Where? Newark, N.J.
11. Where was NOBLE DREW ALI born? In the State of North Carolina.
12. What is his nationality? Moorish-American.
13. What is your nationality? Moorish-American.
14. Why are we Moorish Americans? Because we are descendants of Moroccans and born in America.
15. For what purpose was the Moorish Science Temple of founded? For the uplifting of fallen humanity.

16. How did the Prophet being to uplift the Moorish-Americans? By teaching them to be themselves.
17. What is our religion? Islamism.
18. Is that a new, or is that the old time religion? Old time religion.
19. What kind of a flag is the Moorish? It is a red flag with a five pointed green star in the center.
20. What do the five points represent? Love, Truth, Peace, Freedom, and Justice.
21. How old is our flag? It is over 10,000 years old.
22. Which is our Holy Day? Friday.
23. Why? Because Friday is the day on which man was formed in flesh, and it was on Friday when He departed out of flesh.
24. Who was Jesus? He was a Prophet of Allah.
25. Where was he born? In Bethlehem of Judah, in the House of David.
26. Who were His Father and Mother? Joseph and Mary.
27. Will you give in brief the line (genealogy) through which Jesus came? Some of the Great Fathers through which Jesus came are Abraham, Boaz by Ruth, Jesse, King David, Solomon; Hezekiah and Joseph by Mary.
28. Why did ALLAH send Jesus to this earth? To save the Israelites from the iron-hand oppression of the pale skin nations of Europe who were governing a portion of Palestine at that time.
29. How long has that been? About two thousand years ago.
30. What was the nationality of Ruth? Ruth was a Moabitess.
31. What is the modern name for the Moabites? Moroccans.
32. Where is the Moroccan Empire? Northwest Amexem.
33. What is the modern name for Amexem? Africa.
34. What is the title given to our ruler in Morocco? Sultan.
35. Where do we get the name Jesus? From the East.

36. What does the name Jesus mean? Jesus means Justice.
37. Did the Angel give to the Child that was called Jesus a Holy Name? Yes, but it cannot be used by those who are slaves to sin.
38. What is an Angel? An Angel is a thought of ALLAH manifested in human flesh.
39. What are Angels used for? To carry messages to the four corners of the world, to all nations.
40. What is our Prophet to us? He is an Angel of ALLAH, who is sent to bring us the Everlasting Gospel of ALLAH.
41. What is the Everlasting Gospel? It is a Saving Power that comes from ALLAH through our Ancient Fathers, by His Prophet.
42. What is the Covenant of the Great-GOD-ALLAH? Honor thy Father and thy Mother that thy days may be long upon the Earthland which the Lord thy GOD-ALLAH hath given thee.
43. At what age did Jesus begin to teach? At the age of twelve.
44. Where did He teach? India, Africa and Europe.
45. How long did He teach? Eighteen years.
46. What did Jesus say would make you free? TRUTH.
47. What is TRUTH? TRUTH is Aught
48. What is Aught? Aught is ALLAH.
49. Can TRUTH change? TRUTH cannot change or pass away.
50. What other name do we give to TRUTH? HOLY BREATH.
51. What have you to say about the HOLY BREATH? All we can say is it is great. It is good. It was, it is, and evermore to be. Amen.
52. At what place on earth was the physical part of man formed? In the Garden of Eden.
53. Where is the Garden of Eden? In the land of Canaan, in the City of Mecca.
54. What is the modern name for the Garden of Eden? MECCA.

55. What is the name of the first Physical Man? His name cannot be used, only by Executive Rulers of the A.C. of the M.S.T. of A.
56. What are the words of A.C. of the M.S.T. of A. Adept Chamber of the Moorish Science Temple of America. (3rd Heaven).
57. Who were Adam and Eve? They are the mothers and fathers of the human family. Asiatics and Moslems.
58. Where did they go? They went into Asia.
59. What is the modern name given to their children? Asiatics.
60. Who is guarding the Holy City of MECCA today to keep the unbelievers away? Angels.
61. What is the modern name for those Angels? Asiatics.
62. What is the shade of their skin? Olive.
63. Are the Moorish-Americans any relation to those angels? Yes, we all have the same father and mother.
64. Give five names that are given to the descendants of Adam and Eve: Lucifer, Satan, Devil, Dragon and Beast.
65. What is the Devil sometimes called? The Lower-self.
66. How many selves are there? Two?
67. Name them. Higher-self and Lower-self.
68. What people represent the Higher-self? The Angels who protect the Holy City of MECCA.
69. What people represent the Lower-self? Those who were cast out of the Holy City and those who accept their teaching.
70. What is the Higher-self? The Higher-self is the Mother of the Virtues and the harmonies of life, and breeds Justice, Mercy, Love and Right.
71. Can the Higher-self pass away? No.
72. Why? Because it is ALLAH in MAN.
73. What does the Lower-self breed? Hatred, Slander, Lewdness, Murders, Theft, and everything that harms.

74. What did the Higher-self say to the Lower-self at one time when he met him? Where are you going Satan?

75. What was the answer the Lower-self gave to the Higer-self? I am going to and fro the earth seeking whom I may devour.

76. Has He finished his task of devouring? Yes.

77. When was His time declared out? When He nailed Jesus on the cross.

78. What are the last words Jesus uttered? It is finished.

79. What did He have reference to? He had reference to the end of Satan.

80. Did Jesus say that He would return to conquer Him? Yes.

81. What is the name of the person into whom Jesus was first reincarnated? Prophet MOHAMMAD the Conqueror.

82. Was Satan to be bound then? Satan was to be bound in part.

83. When was the head of Satan taken off? 1453 (Byzantine).

84. By whom? Mohammad.

85. Name some of the marks that were put upon the Moors of Northwest, by the European nations in 1774. Negro, Black, Colored and Ethiopia.

86. What is meant by the word Negro? Negro, a name given to a river in West Africa by the Moors because it contains black water.

87. What is meant by the word Black? Black, according to science means death.

88. What does the word Colored mean? Colored means anything that has been painted, stained, varnished or dyed.

89. What does Ethiopia mean? Ethiopia means something divided.

90. Can a man be a Negro, Black, Colored or Ethiopian? No.

91. Why? Because man is made in the image and after the Likeness of God, Allah.

92. What title does Satan give himself? God.

93. Will you define the word White? White means Purity, Purity means God, and God means the Ruler of the Land.
94. To whom do we refer to at times, as being the GREAT GOD? ALLAH.
95. Is the devil made in the Image and Likeness of ALLAH? No, he is a shadow of our lower-selves and will pass away.
96. Who made the Devil? Elohim.
97. Who is Elohim? Elohim is the Seven Creative Spirits that created everything that ever was, is, and evermore to be.
98. What is Elohim sometimes called? The SEVEN EYES OF ALLAH.
99. How many days are in a Circle? Seven days.
100. How many days are in creation? Seven days.
101. According to Science, how many days are in a year? Seven days.

Questionnaire and Additional Laws For The Moorish Americans

(BY THE PROPHET NOBLE DREW ALI)

ACT 1. Grand Sheiks, and Governors and heads of all Temples, all Business: Each said Temple must be approved by the Prophet Noble Drew Ali. Before acting upon any members, let it be finance, property or any line of life that will cause the members to sacrifice finance, etc., that will cause support of any group of members. Any former officer that violates these laws is subject to be removed from his office under a heavy restriction, etc., by the Prophet or the Grand Sheik.

ACT 2. All members are to attend their adept meetings and their pubic meetings promptly. If a member is found standing around on their meeting period, shall be fined 50c on the first case, and on the second he will be fined one dollar ($1.00), which will go on your emergency fund. If a member is working his monthly dues must be paid, and if he has money in the bank he must subscribe as much as he is able to the Moorish Uplifting Fund, because it takes finance to uplift a Nation.

ACT 3. It is the lawful and divine duty of every good member if he is able in finance to aid me in saving the nation and if he does not, he is an enemy to the cause of uplifting his own people and Justice must catch you. Let it be he or she according to Love, Truth, Peace, Freedom and Justice as I have the power invested in my hands and I will have to enforce the law in order to save the Nation.

ACT 4. All members while up making a public speech must not use any assertion against the American flag or speak radical against the church or any member of any organized group, because we are to teach Love, Truth, Peace, Freedom and Justice

ACT 5. All members must promptly attend their meetings and send their children to Sunday School, and the teacher must confirm himself to the questionary. And let every member exercise his five senses who is able to do so, because out from Sunday School comes the guiders of the Nation.

ACT 6. With us all members must proclaim their nationality and we are teaching our people their nationality and their Divine Creed that they may know that they are a part and parcel of this said government, and know that they are not Negroes, Colored Folks, Black People or Ethiopians, because these names were given to slaves by slave holders in 1779 and lasted until 1865 during the time of slavery, but this is a new era of time now, and all men now must proclaim their free national name to be recognized by the government in which they live and the nations of the earth, this is the reason why Allah the Great God of the Universe ordained Noble Drew Ali, the Prophet to redeem his people from their sinful ways. The Moorish Americans are descendants of the ancient Moabites who inhabited the North Western and South Western shores of Africa.

ACT 7. All members must promptly attend their meetings and become a part and parcel to all uplifting acts of the Moorish Science Temple of America. Members must pay their dues and keep in line with all necessities of the Moorish Science Temple of America then you are entitled to the name of, "Faithful." Husband, you must support your wife and children. Wife, you must obey your husband and take care of your children and look after the duties of your household. Sons and daughters must obey father and mother and be industrious and become a part of the uplifting of fallen humanity. All Moorish Americans must keep their hearts and minds pure with love, and their bodies clean with water. This Divine Covenant is from your Holy Prophet Noble Drew Ali, through the guidance of his Father, God Allah.

The Great Meeting Is On!
ISLAM
ASIA
Koran Questions For Moorish Americans
HUMANITY
PROPHET DREW ALI
THE CARES OF THE WORLD
SALVATION
NOBLE DREW ALI, Founder of
The Moorish Science Temple of America
3140 Indiana Avenue Chicago, Ill., U. S. A.
PRICE 25 CENTS

IV. Koran Questions for Moorish Americans: *102s and 114s*

Source:

Noble Drew Ali, Prophet, "102s / 114s" in *Koran Questions for Moorish Americans: 101s (Also Includes the 102s/ 114s),* revised by G.S. Heru Ranesi-El, 9-11. Atlanta: Moorish Science Temple of America, n.d.

Islam.

The Holy Prophet Noble Drew Ali (El Hajj Sharif Abdul Ali) arranged the "Koran Questions for Moorish Americans" to introduce the Moorish Americans to the truth about themselves. This Questionnaire, also known as the "101s," were preceded by the "102s," although the amount of "keys," or lessons we possess total number 114. While the 102s/ 114s read similarly, they contain keys not mentioned in the more widely distributed 101s.

So as not to violate Act 5 of our Divine Constitution and Bylaws, these lessons are being offered as a supplement to the 101s and we therefore suggest you familiarize yourself with those lessons first and foremost.

Peace

Key 1 –20 read the same as in the 101s

21. How old is our flag? 50,000 years old.

Key 22 –57 read the same as in the 101s

58. Who were Adam and Eve? They are the ones who brought about a discord in the Holy City of Mecca and were cast out.
59. Where did they go? They went into Europe.
60. What was the nationality of the people that cast them out? The Ancient Moabites.
61. How far did they have to travel? Two thousand, two hundred miles across the hot burning desert.
62. How did they travel? Under the pressure of the sword.
63. Who rode and who walked? The Moors rode camels and the Europeans walked and rode goats.
64. What is the modern name given to their children of today? Romans.

65. What is the shade of their skin? Pale.

66. Who is guarding the Holy City of MECCA to keep them from re-entering? Angels.

67. What is the modern name of those Angels? Arabians.

68. What is the shade of their skin? Olive.

69. Are the Moorish Americans any relation to those Angels? Yes, we all have the same mother and father.

70. What is the Title of the Original Royal House of the original Arabians? The House of SAADI.

71. Who are the original Arabs? The Ancient Moabites.

72. How is this? They are the founders of the Holy City of MECCA.

73. Is there a difference between the Arabians and the Arabs of today? Yes, the modern Arabs are strangely mixed descendants of Eve and the Asiatic family.

74. Who are the descendants of Adam and Eve kin today? Distant cousins of the human family, the Asiatic and Moslem.

Key 75 –94 read the same as in the 101s.

95. By whom? Mohammad II.

Key 96 –97 read the same as in the 101s.

98. What is it called today? It is called the River Al Niger. It travels Northwest to Northeast in South America.

99. In reality, what is a Negro? Negro is an animal that has four legs.

Key 100 –114 read the same as in the 101s— these are the keys intercepted in the 102s/ 114s.

"I Am A Citizen of the U.S.A."

V. Divine Constitution & ByLaws of the Moorish Science Temple of America

Noble Drew Ali, Prophet, 1926.

Revised 2013 by Sis. Tauheedah S. Najee-Ullah El.

Historian, Moorish Science Temple California, Inc.

Managing Editor, Califa Media®

Reformatted for inclusion in this text.

Salvation Allah Unity

The Moorish Science Temple of America

THE DIVINE CONSTITUTION AND BY-LAWS

Noble Drew Ali
Founder

ACT 1: The Grand Sheik and the chairman of the Moorish Science Temple of America is in power to make law and enforce laws with the assistance of the Prophet and the Grand Body of the Moorish Science Temple of America. The Assistant Grand Sheik is to assist the Grand Sheik in all affairs if he lives according to Love, Truth, Peace, Freedom, and Justice, and it is known before the members of the Moorish Science Temple of America.

ACT 2: All meetings are to be opened and closed promptly according to the Circle Seven and Love, Truth, Peace, Freedom, and Justice. Friday is our Holy Day of rest, because on a Friday the first man was formed in flesh and on a Friday the first man departed out of flesh and ascended unto his father God, Allah, for that cause Friday is the Holy Day for all Moslems all over the world.

ACT 3: Love, Truth, Peace, Freedom, and Justice must be proclaimed and practiced by all members of the Moorish Science Temple of America. No member is to put in danger or accuse falsely his brother or sister on any occasion at all that may harm his brother or sister, because Allah is Love.

Act 4: All members must preserve these Holy and Divine laws, and all members must obey the laws of the government, because by being a Moorish American, you are a part and parcel of the government, and must live the life accordingly.

Act 5: This organization of the Moorish Science Temple of America is not to cause any confusion or to overthrow the laws and constitution of the said government but to obey hereby.

Act 6: With us all members must proclaim their nationality and we are teaching our people their nationality and their divine creed that they may know that they are a part and a parcel of this said government, and know that they are not Negroes, Colored Folks, Black People, or Ethiopians, because these names were given to slaves by slave holders in 1779 and lasted until 1865 during the time of slavery, but this is a new era of time now, and all men now must proclaim their free national name to be recognized by the government in which they live and the nations of the earth, this is the reason why Allah the Great God of the universe ordained Noble Drew Ali, the Prophet to redeem his people from their sinful ways. The Moorish Americans are the descendants of the ancient Moabites whom inhabited the North Western and South Western shores of Africa.

Act 7: All members must promptly attend their meetings and become a part and a parcel of all uplifting acts of the Moorish Science Temple of America. Members must pay their dues and keep in line with all necessities of the Moorish Science Temple of America, then you are entitled to the name of "Faithful." Husband, you must support your wife and children; wife, you must obey your husband and take care of your children and look after the duties of your household. Sons and daughters must obey father and mother and be industrious and become a part of the uplifting of fallen humanity. All Moorish Americans must keep their hearts and minds pure with love, and their bodies clean with water. This Divine Covenant is from your Holy Prophet Noble Drew Ali, through the guidance of his Father God Allah.

MOORISH AMERICAN PRAYER

Allah the Father of the universe, the Father of Love, Truth, Peace, Freedom and Justice. Allah is my protector, my guide, and my salvation by night and by day, through his Holy Prophet Drew Ali. "Amen."

THE MOORISH SCIENCE TEMPLE OF AMERICA

Home Office: 37th & Federal St. Chicago, IL U.S.A.

VI. Divine Warnings from the Prophet

Source:

Noble Drew Ali, Prophet, "Humanity," in "*I'm Going to Repeat Myself*": *A Compilation of Artifacts Authored by Noble Prophet Drew Ali & The M.S.T. of A.*, edited by Sis. Tauheedah S. Najee-Ullah El, 4-13. Redondo Beach, CA: Califa Media, 2014.

G.S. Salaam El, Rami "Moorish Letters, Documents and Statements," in *Moorish Jewels: Emerald Edition,* 12-24. Redondo Beach, CA: Califa Media, 2014.

To Be Proclaimed in Every Meeting

Islam,

I am glad to know that I have a few faithful Moors among you all, and I desire for them to know the Truth, and the Divine Truth. There is a host of Jealousy, about Me, and the Movement now by the same people of our side of the Nation that claim that I was only a joke and unreal; but now since they have found out from the Government Officials and the Nations of the Earth, that this is the only Soul Foundation that all Asiatics must depend upon for their Earthly Salvation as American Citizens. They are working every scheme that they can to disqualify Me so they may take charge of the situation.

I have notified all these things to you long ago in the past. It is through the faithful Moors that attribute to the Movement and Uplifting Funds; the ones that paid their Divine respect to Me and the Movement, will be remembered. That is why I am calling Upon all faithful Moors to increase their faithfulness to Me, Your Prophet, and Your Divine Moorish Movement.

I need finance, and I need it badly. Never before have I needed Finance so badly as I do at present so I can shove aside the Discord that is facing the Nation. It all comes through Jealousy, Because of My Fame and Nobility. The Nations of the World will not recognize the movement without I, The PROPHET, being Head. It has been proven by My works, which I have performed in the past few Years.

A Warning From the Prophet
To Be Read in Every Meeting

I, hereby inform all members that they must end all radical speeches while at work in their homes or on the streets. We are for peace and not destruction. Stop flashing your cards at Europeans; it causes confusion. Remember your card is for your salvation. Failure to obey these orders will be of severe consequence.

We are for Love, Truth, Peace, Freedom, and Justice, and when these principles are violated, justice must then take its course.

Any member or group of members who hold malicious feelings toward the temple or the Prophet, or violate the divine covenant of the Moorish Movement will receive their reward from Allah for their unjust deeds.

All true Moors will and must obey the law as laid down to them by their Prophet. If they lose confidence in their Prophet, they should turn in their card and button, cease wearing their turban and fez and return to the state where I, the Prophet, found you.

This is a holy and divine movement founded by the Prophet Noble Drew Ali, and if the Prophet is not right, the temple is not right.

The Prophet, therefore, is sending out the divine plea to all Moorish Americans that they do their part in protecting their Prophet and the Temple.

This is an everlasting movement founded by the Prophet through the will of "Allah" to redeem his people from their sinful ways.

To the Members of The Moorish Science Temple of America

Islam,

This is the instruction from your Prophet Noble Drew Ali.

Be faithful unto your Forefathers Divine, and National Creed, that You will be blessed for your good deeds, that You sow in the flesh. "ALLAH" is the one that judges the World, and His judgment is now on. But the weak can comprehend it not. The end of Time is drawing near, so says "ALLAH" to His Divine "PROPHET I Noble Drew ALI". And that's why many hearts have been turned to stone, and many have Eyes to see, But cannot see, Ears to hear, But cannot hear. Least they would be confounded of their sins.

These are the trying hours now dear Moors, and every evil spirit is moving, And they are trying every weak mind, to overthrow and drag out the true foundation, that has been laid, and to cause confusion in the minds of the ones that do believe. But if you have the true Love of "ALLAH" and the spirit of your Forefathers, you fear not what you hear or see; but will sacrifice the utmost of your very life to protect your Movement and your "PROPHET." Watch your Enemies dear Moors; your enemies are the ones that speak against your "PROPHET," and ridicule

Him to the very lowest and the ones that speak against "Your Divine and National Principles of Your Temples." Act accordingly, and "ALLAH" will bless you for your good work, "PEACE."

Prophet Makes Plea to Nation

Our Divine and National Movement stands for the specific grand principles of Love, Truth, Peace, Freedom, and Justice, and I, The Prophet, am applying to all loyal, faithful Moors, members, and the American citizens to help me in my great uplifting acts of uplifting fallen humanity among the Asiatic race and nation, for I have suffered much and severely in the past through misunderstanding of what the movement was dedicated to.

It is the Great God Allah alone that guides the destiny of this Divine and National Movement. I know all true American citizens are identified by national descent names to answer and apply to the free national constitution of this free National Republic of the United States of America. That's why I am calling on all true national citizens to help me morally and financially in my great work I am doing to help this national government. For without a free national name, without a descent flag of your forefathers, there is not a national divine title of the government in which we live.

This is from your true and Divine Prophet unto all American and foreign sympathizers.

The Voice of the Prophet

If you have race pride and love your race, join the Moorish Science Temple of America and become a part of this Divine Movement, then you will have the power to redeem your race because you will know who you are, and your forefather were. Because where there is unity there is strength. “Together we stand, divided we fall.”

Come, good people, because I, the Prophet, sent to redeem this nation from mental slavery, which you have now, need every one of you who think that your condition can be better. This is a field open to strong men and women to uplift the nation and take your place in the affairs of men.

If the Europeans and other nations are helping me, why not you? It is your problem. The Negro problem is being solved only as it can, and that is by the Moorish National Divine Movement. If you have a nation you must have a free national name in order to be recognized by this nation as an American citizen. This is what was meant when it said, "Seek ye first the kingdom of Heaven and all these things would be added unto you."

Religious Controversy

In this age there is still much religious controversy as to the right thing.

Big and powerful ministers have come to the conclusion that something is wrong. Some say it is the Ten Commandments, others say there is a lack of sincerity in the purpose of the churches; still others think it is all worthless and not fit for the time it takes to attend them. However or whatever their final decision might be, it is certain they will make a change or rather try to make one.

The fact of the matter is that they have always had only a reflection of the truth and not the real thing. Like one who holds up to the sun a mirror and casts a few of its diverted rays in a different direction, so have they done with the truth that is supposed to have come from the East.

There are but few people who know what the truth is about man, and that few know that it is foolish to try to impart it to the ignorant. Although the ignorant has finished college, he is a fool right on, being trained to jump through a hoop. The longer he stays in the schools, the better he can jump, and the more he defends his jumping.

From the East comes all light, but though the sun is hanging at high noon; the blind cannot see. The same as the Islamic Creed from the East was brought to the Asiatics of America by the Prophet, NOBLE DREW ALI, and offered to those who were sick at heart, tried for many years, yet they are blind and cannot see the light, Nor is the Prophet trying to put new wine in old skins, for he knows that it will burst them. Still he has the only remedy for the nations. The remedy brought by Jesus, Mohammed, Confucius, and all of the other prophets, which remedy is truth.

The nations do not want the truth; it is too stern, but until they accept it and find out where it is, there will continue to be religious controversy.

Savior of Humanity

In this electrified age men are racing into this life without complete knowledge of where they are going, or what the end will be, when riches seem to be their only pursuit, to be obtained anyway and at any cost; when selfishness, avarice, greed and lust dominate their very being; when humanity in general is left at the mercy of those who have no mercy in them. It is truly wonderful and astounding to see one come into this mad human drama for the sole purpose of saving humanity. Losing all sight on those things worldly and yielding absolutely to a cause higher than has ever yet been attained. This picture is the likeness of Prophet Noble Drew ALI who is serving humanity.

Coming as he does with a message for the nations in somewhat the same manner as did Jesus, Mohammed, Buddha, Confucius and other prophets of their day. Only the things of this prophet's day differ from the ills of the days of the past; and yet the remedy for the ills of today is about the same as the remedies for the days past; all turning about the pivot Love -love for humanity.

Humanity must be lifted from the unwholesome depths of poverty, misery and suffering and placed on the solid rock of salvation. There are some who claim to do this but upon investigation, one finds that they have slouched under the wings of their cross to extract from those who come to them, means by which they can have the pleasures of this life, while they point their followers to joy after death. While they "feed their sheep" they also shear them while eating. At the close of their day the Master will be heard to tell them, "You have your reward, get thee hence."

Rare is it that you find a real prophet whose mission is the salvation of the nations. The land is full of false prophets whose mission is to fleece the people.

The time was and now is that there should come into the land a prophet in the likeness of his brothers, to redeem them from sin and slavery. Truly this Prophet Noble Drew Ali is the man, bringing with him the message of Love, Truth, Peace, Freedom, and Justice. which alone can save the nations. Like the coming of Jesus, he does not come from the elect, nor the rich, nor the mighty in worldly power, but all power is given unto him to do good. This power is from Allah.

It will be his works that will make men of every nation accept the truth that he brings. It will be through his teachings that the nations of the earth will understand the will of the Master; it will be through him that "Peace on earth and good will to all men" shall come. It will be through his work that humanity will be brought from the slime of life and placed on the solid rock of salvation.

Caveat Emptor

Moors are men, upright, independent and fearless who care for their loved ones and follow the Prophet to a destiny which is not uncertain nor unknown. They are fortified by the impregnable doctrine built upon Love, Truth, Peace, Freedom and Justice. It is therefore, folly at its greatest height for smelly culprits with their insidious plans to invade such realm.

They try and try but their own bad planning brings down wrath upon their heads like the sword old Damocles had. Intrigue and scurrilous cunnings find a difficult path to travel within the ranks of the Moors. This is so because the Moorish Movement has been well planned by Prophet Noble Drew Ali, whose latent powers are abundant, unknown and may be called into action, as a matter of defense, at any moment.

Prophet Noble Drew Ali knows the people within his ranks who are interested. They are the vanguard of the Movement as the Moorish hordes increase here in America. All of the Moors are active not passive. A member's interest can only be in one direction and having traveled over the road years before the Prophet knows where every member is along the road.

A few feet below is another road where schemers work, where traitors grin, and culprits bask in the sun. They think they are on the same road with true Moors, but the Moors are high above on a pinnacle where they might view the destructionists as they fall for the last time and their bones bleach in the sultry mid-day sun.

Hungry scavengers flying high, catch scent, devour and leave crying out: Caveat Emptor - - cast out the dead carcass. The Moors high above see these plotters, purveyors, the worst that exist, hurl themselves downward by their own works as the hawks wait.

Prophet Announces His Authority & Power

Forced to make changes. All Governors and other officers of the Moorish Science Temple are hereby congratulated for their past loyalty and fidelity, for I know it will be the same in the future. Because of certain incidents that have arisen in some of the Temples which seem to come from the fact that there are those who do not know where the seat of power is vested the Prophet has ordered the following to be published;

All authority and power of the Moorish Science Temple of America is vested in the Prophet Noble Drew Ali and those whom he appoints to act as in the Supreme Body. The Prophet has the authority and power to expel any officer or member of the Moorish Science Temple of America who willfully violates or refuses to comply with the rules in regard to branch Moorish Science Temple and such suspensions and expulsions shall stand until in the judgment of the Prophet, the members and officers shall have made satisfactory atonement. All officers and members of the Moorish Science Temple of America and such rules and regulations of the constitution shall be in writing and not at variance with any law of the city, town or nation which the prophet shall declare a law.

During this session of the convention, all rules, regulations, and laws of the constitution and such as might be enacted and ordered by the Prophet, shall express and explain in detail, so there can be no doubt as to what is required of each and every officer or member of the organization.

The Prophet will positively not tolerate any interference with the operation of this National Divine Movement from anyone.

A Warning from the Prophet

For All Governors, Grand Sheiks, and Head Officials of All Temples
Friday, October 26th, 1928

Renew your acts, amend your ways. Because the great conference is on its way and in it is where the Law will be enforced before the great grand body. The continuance of the present officers in the temple will depend on your past good work. Those who have been delinquent may now know that they will not be tolerated any longer, because this great Divine and National movement must move on according to Law, these things shall be proclaimed.

There is no favorite in any of the temples, for the Law is laid down and everyone who claims a part of the work must be governed accordingly. ALL are one. There is but one Temple in this Nation and there is but one Prophet of the Temples. I come to speak to all Nations, bringing them a message of Love, Truth, Peace, freedom, and Justice. In the Head of every Temple if any one has violated these Divine Laws it will mean his discontinuance, for no man is to be under the influence of intoxicating liquors nor to seek to tear up the families while under the influence of evil motive; nor must he speak anything that will prejudice the minds of the public against the Divine movement.

If any of the Laws are violated, any body grand sheik or sheiks can file charge against the violation to the grand body over which the Prophet presides. This power is vested in seven or more sheiks for the protection of your Temple and the Divine movement.

The Prophet Has Spoken

All Governors and Grand Sheiks and head officials that guide any body of Moors of any Temple of the Moorish Science Temple of America:

He or she must be of good moral standard and a heart of love and their works must be of Love, Truth, Peace, Freedom and Justice. They are to imitate the Prophet in speech and teaching in any said Temple. They must not be under the influence of intoxicating liquors or any other harmful motive that will terminate to become detrimental to the organization. It must not be known that any leader is staying away from home or neglecting his duty at home or must allow the public to know of their wrong doings. They must forever live the life of Love at home and it must be known by all the members. They must not speak rash words nor any profane language in the mildest form to any other individual because a leader without influence of good works cannot be a leader, and to be a real Moorish leader you must study the Koran and the Divine Constitution that is handed down unto you by I, the Prophet.

No finance business is to be opened with any group of members of any Temple, by the Governor or Grand Sheik or whosoever in charge without the consultation of I, the Prophet. All uplifting funds, books, are to be issued only through I, the Prophet, because that money is to finance the Moorish Movement.

The head of any Temple can maintain an emergency fund which cannot exceed the amount of from 25 cents to 50 cents a week per member. All public collections and dues also to the supporting of each said Temple and its domestic work.

No finance books are to be served in any Temple except by the Prophet. The head of every Temple must by law obey the word of the Prophet, and if any leader or head of any Temple fails to obey these laws - embezzlement is his charge, and is subject to enforcement of the law by the Grand Body. And the penalty may be a fine or a removal from office, or placed under a very heavy restriction of the law.

Think This Over, You Moors

All Sheiks, Grand Sheiks must prepare for the Prophet before he comes to visit them. Must see to it that all is clean and in perfection as far as comfort is possible, or otherwise don't arrange to have his presence. All members should pay from 25 cents to 50 cents weekly towards the Emergency Fund. This fund will increase so that it will soon amount to the grand sum of $1,000. That is, if you are loyal Moors. The Emergency Fund goes into the bank. The treasurer will tend to the responsibility of seeing that the money is in the bank, yes, and under the name of the Moorish Science Temple of America Finance. When needed, act according to the law pertaining to the procedure of performing an Emergency Act.

No head of any said Temple is to borrow from any member more than five to ten dollars unless by notification of the Prophet, the necessity for the loan. When any said Temple desires to purchase property they must first notify the Grand Body or the Prophet and it must be purchased under the name of the Moorish Science Temple of America or Noble Drew Ali. An individual name should never be applied. I, Noble Drew Ali, am responsible for all finance, so therefore let I, the Prophet, know what is on me.

Some of you have slipped and slipped drastically, so you had better lace up your shoes before I get there. Everything, every business transaction or anything pertaining to finance is to be transacted in the name of the Moorish Science Temple of America, or Noble Drew Ali. We Moors must maintain a grand treasurer, just as in the days of our forefathers; then you are a nation-until then, you are nothing.

The Emergency Fund is issued by no book, but by an emergency card punched according to contribution, then marked on book; that is the law, and the law must live. The government is behind me, and I must get behind you. For I must uphold and enforce the law, my mission is to save you Moors.

The heads of all Temples, Grand Sheiks, Grand Sheikesses must confirm to the Divine principles: Love, Truth, Peace, Freedom, and Justice. They must live the life among the members and be loved even as the Prophet is loved. They must not practice the principle of segregation among any group in his or her Temple. Let it be he or she that is head of any Temple of the Moorish Science Temple of America that if there should come any grievance that cannot be settled by the head, notify the Prophet at once.

No member is to attend Adept Chamber that has not lived a moral and clean life, and has not paid his or her dues or assessments, providing that he or she is working or able, cannot consider himself a Moor. But traitors must be excluded from the books after having fair trial by the head of their Temple, and that must be sent into the Grand Body. And all members that are able to, subscribe towards the uplifting fund because it takes finance to uplift a nation. And those that are able and fail to act, are not Moors, but traitors to their cause and trust and their nation, and are not allowed to share all the Moorish honors. And the penalty is-- It is embezzlement of the faith of our creed. All heads of all Temples must observe these laws.

Divine Warning by Prophet Noble Drew Ali
General Laws

Every Temple and head is to function by words, deeds, and actions, imitating the Prophet. Especially when teaching a group of Moors, any group of Moors.

These are the General Laws--- the Supreme laws will be handed you to-morrow night. The Supreme Council will be chosen to-morrow, consisting of seven men, tried and true, accepted by you according to their words, works and deeds.

The head of all temples are to give an account once a month of all finances into the Grand Body. and the Grand Sheik---Grand Sheikess---Governor, and Grand Governor of any said Temple are to work hand in hand and intercede that the Prophet is the Law. They are to know they are a part of the law and must obey.

The Heads of all Temples are to by force refrain from all wrath words profanity in the mildest form from his members. They must live the life of Love, Truth, Peace, Freedom, and Justice, and refrain from all alcoholic liquors or any other harmful things that will terminate to destroy Peace, or any other of the Divine Principles. They are not to contribute to anything that will cause the public to disagree with he or she. And for one to lead a group of Moors, you must keep your house clean - - clean with good deeds, kind words-your wives, brothers must hear good words, kind words, and must know of your good deeds. If there are children you must see to their support. Follow this Divine Principle, for if you don't restrict to this Divine Principle then you are not a true Moor, and the heads are not to charge for membership, or to overcharge for cards, buttons, or for anything issued by the Prophet. Those who contribute to either of the preceding are not Moors, but robbers.

Membership, sisters and brothers, is free; not only here but all over the world. The button is 25 cents, card 25 cents; and one month's dues is paid. Every member pays 50 cents a month for dues. This money goes towards the support of the Temple. This, if not paid, does not entitle you to the protection that is provided for you and especially if you are not working or in the position to work. If you neglect to fulfill this small duty assigned you. how can you rightfully expect money or other help when you are sick or otherwise disabled.

And to be a real Moorish leader you must study the Koran and the Divine constitution that is handed down unto you by I, the Prophet.

The head of any Temple can maintain an emergency fund which can not exceed the amount of from twenty-five cents to fifty cents a week per member. All public collections and dues also go to the support of the Temple and its domestic work. The head of every Temple must, by law, obey the word of the Prophet, and if any head leader or head of any Temple fails to obey these laws -embezzlement is his charge and is subject to enforcement of the law by the Grand Body: and the penalty may be a fine or removal from office, or being placed under a very heavy restriction of the law.

Prophet Sends Marriage Law to All Temples

All marriage ceremonies of members of the Moorish Science Temple of America must be performed by an ordained minister and the head of the temple.

And any man desiring to take unto himself a wife and receive our Moorish rites, he must go to the City Hall and receive his license to be registered in that city, county, and state. It then must be turned over in the hands of the aforesaid ordained minister and head of a temple after it has been properly signed by city officials. The price thereby for such administering to man and wife will be five dollars. For all those who have their papers and desire our Moorish marriage ceremony, it is three dollars.

We Moors cannot marry no one but we obligate you according to our divine laws and covenant and the laws of the land. This must be proclaimed and made known to every temple so that there will be no misunderstanding. There will be no misunderstanding about I, the Prophet, and my teachings because Allah alone binds two hearts together as a unit. These are the marriage obligations and instructions for man and wife:

Chapter 22 from our Koran is to be read first to the husband and chapter 21 is to be read secondly to the wife. These are the instructions of marriage from our Holy Koran. Please obey the law as given you by your Prophet through your Governor.

The Industrious Acts of the Moslems

Moorish Guide of Friday, December 15, 1928.

These are the Moabites, Hamathites, Canaanites who were driven out of the land of Canaan by Joshua, and received permission of the Pharaohs of Egypt to settle in that portion of Egypt. In later years they formed themselves kingdoms. These kingdoms are called this day Morocco, Algiers, Tunis, Tripoli, etc.

They originated the beauties of the Alhambra and to an unpracticed eye the light relives and fanciful arabesques which cover the walls of the Alhambra appear to have been sculptured by the hand. With a minute and patient labor, and inexhaustible variety of detail, yet a general uniformity and harmony of design truly astonishing. And this may especially be said of the vaults, and cupolas which are wrought like honeycombs or frost work, with stalactites, and pendants which confound the beholder with the seeming intricacy of their patterns. The astonishment ceases, however, when it is discovered that this is all stucco work, plates of plaster of paris cast in moulds and skillfully joined so as to form patterns of every size and form. This mode of disappearing walls with arabesques and stuccoing the vaults with grotto work was invented in Damascus but highly improved by the Moors in Morocco to whom Saracenic architecture owes its most graceful and fanciful details. The process by which all this fairy tracery was produced was ingeniously simple. The walls in their naked state were divided off by lines crossing at right angles, such as artists use in copying a picture. Over these were drawn a succession of interesting regiments of circles. By the aid of these the artists could work with celerity and certainty and from the mere intersection of their plain and curved lines arose the interminable variety of patterns, and the general uniformity of their character. Much gilding was used in the stucco work, especially of the cupolas, and the interstices were delicately penciled with brilliant colors, such as vermilion and lapis lazuli laid on with the whites of eggs.

The primitive colors alone were used, says Ford, by the Egyptians, Greeks, and Arabs, in the early period of art, and they prevail in the Alhambra wherever the artist has been Arabic or Moorish. It is remarkable how much of their original brilliancy remains after the lapse of several centuries. The lower part of the walls in the saloons to the height of several feet is encrusted with glazed tiles, joined like the plates of stucco work so as to form various patterns. On some of these are emblazoned the escutcheons of the Moslem Kings traversed with a band and motto. These glazed tiles, Azzulijas in Spanish, Azzulija in Arabic are of Oriental origin.

Their coolness, cleanliness and freedom from vermin render them admirably fitted in sultry climates for paving halls, and fountains. Encrusting bathing rooms and lining the walls of chambers. Ford is inclined to give them great antiquity. From their prevailing colors, sapphire and blue, he deduces that they may have formed the kind of pavements alluded to in the Sacred Scriptures. "There was under his feet as it were a paved work of sapphire stone," Exod. xxiv-10 and again. "Behold I will lay thy stones with the fairy colors and lay their foundations with sapphires."-Isa. IV-II. These glazed or porcelain tiles were introduced into Spain at an early date by the Moslems. Some are to be seen among the Moorish ruins have been there upwards of eight centuries. Manufactures of them still exist in the Peninsula and they are much used in the Spanish houses, especially in the southern provinces for paving and lining the summer apartments. The Spaniards introduced them into the Netherlands when they had possession ol that country. The people of Holland adopted them with avidity as wonderfully suited to their passion for household cleanliness. And thus these Oriental inventions, the Azzulijas of the Spaniards, the Azzulija if the Arabs, have come to be commonly known as Dutch tiles.

By PROFESSOR DREW, The Egyptian Adept Student.

Moorish Leader's Historical Message to America

In connection with the aims, objects, rules and regulations of the Moorish Science Temple of America. I deem It proper to submit to you a brief statement of our organization, covering Its inception, rise and progress and of the Mohammedan religion, which I hope will be satisfactory to you and be the means of causing you at all times to adhere to the principles of Love, Truth, Peace, Freedom, and Justice in your relations with mankind in general. I further, most anxiously hope this brief statement will help you to more clearly see the duty and wisdom of at all times upholding those fundamental principles which are desired for our civilization of our posterity, such as obedience to law. respect and loyalty to government, tolerance, and unity.

We organized as the Moorish Temple of Science in the year of 1925, and were legally incorporated as a civic organization under the laws of the State of Illinois, November 29th, 1926. The name Moorish Temple of Science changed to the Moorish Science Temple of America, May 1928, in accordance with the legal requirements of the Secretary of the State of Illinois.

The object of our Organization is to help in the great program of uplifting fallen humanity and teach those things necessary to make our members better citizens.

A National organization with a Rotarian complexion as it relates to branch Temples became obvious with the increasing number of inquiries from men and women in different sections of the country concerning the purpose of the organization. There are branch Temples in fifteen (15) different states at this time.

Since the work of the Moorish Science Temple of America was largely religious, the organization has been legally changed to a religious corporation and an affidavit to this effect has been properly filed in the Cook County Recorders office in Illinois.

Inspired by the lofty teachings of the Koran, we have it as the revealed word of God Allah. We shall foster the principles of its teachings among our members. This is our religious privilege as American citizens, under the laws of one of the greatest documents of all time-the American Constitution.

The Mohammedan religion is the least appreciated and probably the most misunderstood of the world's great religions. This is especially true in our western world. Try to understand what Mohammedanism stands for, and some of the things it has contributed to the world.

Mohammed was the founder of the Mohammedan religion. It originated thirteen centuries ago on Arabian Peninsula, where the streams of commerce and culture met and mingled in the middle ages, where the markets of exchange were stationed for treasures of India and the products of the Mediterranean coasts. There, this religion was established in the unprecedented short period of twenty years, and unlike many other religions, without the aid of any royal patronage and support. Buddhism had its Asoka: Judaism its Joshua: Christianity its Constantine: hut Mohammedanism had no person of royal rank and power to assist in its establishment and spread.

Today this religion is acknowledged by nearly two hundred and fifty million souls and extends over an area equal to one-third of the globe. From Arabia it spread eastward over Persia, Turkestan, Afghanistan, westward across Syria, Asia Minor, Turkey; southward to Africa, covering more than half of that continent. It found its way to India, and beyond, to the Islands of Sumatra, Java, and Borneo.

To the early representatives of this faith the world's debt is incalculably great. For it was they who transmitted the treasures of Greek literature from the middle ages to the Renaissance; they who originated the graceful forms of which the Taj Mahal and the Alhambra are the most famous examples. It was they who contributed to the sciences of algebra and chemistry, astronomy, and medicine; they who dotted the Saracen Empire with universities and who built at Bagdad and

Cairo the most renowned universities of the world. During those centuries of ecclesiastical despotism when the Christian church suppressed all intellectual activities save those that were theological, causing the talent that reproduces to supplant the genius that creates. Mohammedans did all in their power to encourage and stimulate research in every branch of human inquiry.

The Moors or Mohammedans added to the beauty and grandeur of Spain. For centuries art, science, literature, and chivalry flourished among them, while the rest of Europe was still sunk in the gloom of the Dark Ages. The Moors were the most ingenious and industrious of the subjects of Spain. Their expulsion from Spain in 1610, was one of the chief causes of decadence of that country, for both agriculture and industry fell into decay after their departure. Mohammedanism makes no distinction between high and low, rich and poor; it is like the sky, it has room for all.

The Koran should be of interest to all readers. It is the Bible of the Mohammedans, ruling over the customs and actions of over 200 millions of people. It is a work of importance whether considered from a religious philosophical, or literary viewpoint.

In the promotion of plans for the betterment of mankind, there has ever been some kind of opposition. And strange as it may seem, such opposition has come from sources where there were no ideas or the lack of courage to force attention to ideas. Whether in church, state or the social community, any attempt to do anything out of the usual way, seldom fails to receive criticism. Not because the course cannot be pursued legally or that it is unreasonable, but because it has been considered in terms as new.

The Moorish Science Temple of America has received some opposition and criticism. In the main the opposition has come from certain Christian ministers. They have expressed themselves as being opposed to our propagation of the Mohammedan religion. Possibly because the promotion of the Mohammedan faith among our people in the United States is considered by them in terms as something new. Whatever the reasons may be for their opposition, the legal right to oppose citizens, individuals and organizations alike for their religious belief does not exist in the United States. The door of religious freedom made by the American Constitution swings open to all, and people may enter through it and worship as they desire. Without religious freedom, no search for truth would be possible; without religious freedom, no discovery of truth would be useful; without religious freedom, religious progress would be checked and we would no longer march forward toward the nobler life which the future holds for the races of men; without religious freedom, there would be no inspiration to lift our heads and gaze with fearlessness into the vast beyond, seeking a hope eternal..

It is a sad weakness in us after all, to oppose our fellowmen for their religious beliefs, and if there are angels who record the sorrows of men as well as their sins, they certainly know how many and deep are the useless sorrows that spring forth from such opposition. Possibly, love and time will cancel our ancient hatreds in this regard and prove that in mankind, tolerance is better than unwarranted opposition.

In connection with our religious aims and beliefs, we must promote economic security. The preaching of economic security among us is by no means as widespread and intensive as the circumstances demand. No other one thing is more needed among us at this time than greater economic, power. Better positions for our men and women, more business employment for our boys and girls and bigger incomes will follow our economic security. We shall be secure in nothing until we have economic power. A beggar people cannot develop the highest in them, nor can they attain to a genuine enjoyment of the spiritualties of life.

Our men, women and children should be taught to believe in the capacity of our group to succeed in business, in spite of the trials and failures of some of them. Trials and failures in business are by no means confined to any particular group of people. Some business ventures of all people fail. We have many men and women among our people who are qualified, both by training and experience, who are shining lights in the business world of all the people. It is a sad weakness in us as a people that we have withheld the very encouragement, support and patronage that would have made some of our worthy business ventures a grand success. And worst of all, have joined in the condemnations of them when they failed. Except in cases of actual dishonesty, discourtesy, lack of service and actual unreliability, our business enterprises in every field of endeavor should have lulled of confidence cooperation and patronage whenever and wherever they can be given.

Read carefully the doctrines of The Moorish Science Temple of America. It contains our hopes, aims, rules and articles of religion. Every member should have a copy.

In conclusion, I urge you to remember there is work enough for all to do in helping to build a better world. The problems of life are largely social and economic. In a profound sense, they are moral and spiritual. Have lofty conceptions of your duties to your country and fellowman in general and especially those with whom you deal. This includes such honesty and righteousness as will cause you to put yourself in the other fellow's place. Look for the best in others and give them the best that is in you. Have a deeper appreciation for womanhood. Brighten the hopes of our youth in order that their courage be increased to dare and do wondrous things. Adhere at all times to the principles of love, truth, peace, freedom, and justice.

I am your affectionate leader. I shall continue to labor day and night, both in public and private, for your good, thereby contributing to the welfare of our country and its people as a whole.

VII. Hadiths & Prophesies of Noble Drew Ali

As hadith are oral statements passed down generationally, there are no original prints to support the proceeding contents. However, after searching for and comparison of the many versions of the Hadith, we have been able to focus on the similarities, and Allah willing, have wound up close to a creditable version of the individual statements.

We have omitted the commentaries usually found with these statements as those are one presenter's view. These statements will resonate with the reader as Allah intended, minus the distraction of the perspective of another. Those wishing to consider the view points of others may access them via the below source list.

(Note: Some of these sayings may have come from others who claimed to be the Prophet Noble Drew Ali especially the quotes without the name of the person citing the Prophet. Please read and propagate this with caution).

Prophesies and Hadiths of Noble Drew Ali: Oral Statements of the Prophet. sevensealspublications.com/

http://www.moorishsciencetemple.org/#!drew alis prophecies and hadiths /c6w1

www.moorishsciencetemple.org/#!blank/c95p

"If you doubt that I am a Prophet, watch my Prophecies" ~ Prophet Drew Ali

1. The Holy Prophet Noble Drew Ali told the Moors, "***I brought you everything it takes to save a nation, take it and save yourself.***" When He said that, the Prophet was holding up a Holy Koran of the Moorish Science Temple of America and a Questionnaire to show us the books we need to save ourselves.
2. The Holy Prophet told the Moors, "***Children, you are at home, and the European is 3,000 miles from home, and he is going to have to take some water***". Reported by Bro. O. Payton Bey, Temple #25, Detroit, Michigan.
3. Bro. I. Cook Bey and other Moors said The Holy Prophet said, "***My good Moors are going to live.***"
4. The Holy Prophet said, "***I am going to stop the European from thinking, and start you [Moors] to thinking for your own good.***"
5. Sister A. Brown El of Temple #25 said that the Holy Prophet said, "***If you got people in the South, get them out, because that is where destruction is going to start.***"
6. The Holy Prophet told The Moors, "***For the various lynchings and murders that were committed in the South; the South is going to have to pay off, and pay off in blood.***"
7. Bro. J. Foster Bey of Temple #4 and #25 said the Holy Prophet would say, "***Every word that I speak is spirit, and you Moors had better heed.***"
8. Bro. G. Cook Bey, Grand Sheik of Temple #1, Chicago, Ill. Said that the Holy Prophet said, "***Look around and where you see people; one day, wild animals will be roaming down the streets.***"
9. Bro. J. Foster Bey, Asst. Grand Sheik of Temple #25 and a member of Temple #4 in the 1920's said that the Holy Prophet said, "***When the fire comes, I will be the water.***"
10. Moors that saw and heard the Holy Prophet said that He said, "***What are all these people doing here. There is only going to be a handful saved. I can count them on my fingers, and have fingers left over.***"
11. Sister M. Payton Bey of Temple 4 and 25 said that the Holy Prophet Noble Drew Ali said, "***I have got airplanes, zeppelins, and apparatus. I am going to take my good***

Moors up in an apparatus on an incline until it's all over with."

12. Bro. B. Jones El of Temple #43 heard the Holy Prophet, say, "***One day, they are going to tear down all the churches and take the bells and melt them down, and make bullets to fight with.***"
13. Bro. J. Blakely Bey said that the Holy Prophet Noble Drew Ali said, "***One day, every wheel of industry is going to stop, and when they start up again, it will be in the Asiatics favor.***"
14. Bro. J. Blakely Bey said that the Holy Prophet said, "***If the European be just, they would have an Asiatic Vice President, and if they had an Asiatic President, they would have a European Vice President.***"
15. Bro. J. Blakely Bey said that the Holy Prophet Noble Drew Ali said, "***In the year 2000, the Moors will come into their own.***"
16. Bro. O. Payton Bey of Temple #4 and #25 said that the Holy Prophet said, "***One day your biggest trouble won't be getting with European women, it will be fighting them off.***"
17. Sister M. Tiggs El of Temple #9 said that the Holy Prophet said, "***When the Europeans go back to Europe, the climate would go back to what it used to be***."
18. Sister M. Tiggs El said that the Holy Prophet told the Moors that "***Before the European came here (to North America), that the bananas were large, and the grapes were four in hand, it took two men with hand sticks to carry one bunch of grapes."***
19. The Holy Prophet told the Moors that "***When destruction comes, I am going to leave enough fine buildings, so that my good Moors will be able to enjoy them.***"
20. Bro. G. Cook Bey, Grand Sheik of Temple #1 said that the Holy Prophet said, "***One day, women are going to be chasing men like a hound running after a rabbit***."
21. Bro. T. Booker Bey, Grand National Treasurer said that the Holy Prophet said, "***The European will not be able to remove all the wealth from the land. After he goes back to Europe, mountains of gold would be revealed to the Moors.***"
22. Bro. B. Jones El of Temple #43 heard the Holy Prophet say, "***Children, you are just plain rich.***"

23. Bro. J. Blakely Bey said that the Holy Prophet said, "***The European is going to have to pay our people off for the work that they did in slavery, and pay off in compounded interest.***"
24. The Holy Prophet told the Moors that "***One day you will go to the store, and there will be soldiers there with guns with bayonets on them, and they will not let you enter. They will order you to move on.***"
25. Bro. I. Cook Bey, Grand Governor of Illinois, said that the Holy Prophet said. "***One day, the Europeans are going to lock the food up in warehouses, put soldiers around them to guard them, and you will go anywhere he says to get something to eat.***"
26. Sister A. Brown El of Temple #4 and #25 said that the Holy Prophet said, "***One day the European is going to let you down. You are going to have to put up a 90 day supply of food to last you until your brothers come to your rescue from the East.***"
27. Bro. R. Wise Bey of Temple #4 and #25 said that the Holy Prophet said, "***One day, some of you old Moors are going to be so hungry that you are going to bite into your own flesh, and blood will skeet out, and you are going to get angry with yourself, because you didn't put up enough food.***"
28. Bro. A. Wise Bey, Grand National Secretary said that the Holy Prophet said, "***I didn't tell anyone where I was born at or who my parents were, because I didn't want people to make a shrine out of the place or make over my parents like was done with Joseph and Mary.***"
29. Bro. T. Booker Bey, Grand National Treasurer said that the Holy Prophet said, "***The Moors were once sea faring people and fed the world, the time is going to come, when we would go back and feed the world again***".
30. The Holy Prophet Noble Drew Ali showed Bro. T. Booker Bey and some other Moors one night, a spot in Chicago, Illinois, where a Moabite Queen ruled from. Her name was Queen Netha (Neith?), and she waged war against five Pharaohs. At that spot, the Holy Prophet dug down into the ground, and pulled up a metal bar with foreign writing on it.
31. Sister M. Tiggs El and other Moors reported that the Holy Prophet said that "***Chicago, Illinois is going to be our new Mecca.***"

32. The Holy Prophet Noble Drew Ali told the Moors that "***Chicago is doomed and Detroit must go down for what they have done to I, your Prophet.***"

33. Sister M. Howell Bey of Temple #19, Flint, Michigan heard the Holy Prophet say, "***One day, grass is going to grow up in Detroit.***"

34. The Holy Prophet told the Moors to "***Try to live close together.***"

35. Bro. J. Foster Bey of Temple #4 and #25 heard the Holy Prophet aid, "***We (The Moors) have the blood of every nation flowing through our veins, thereby bringing about a cross spirit.***"

36. Sister M. Payton Bey of Temple #4 and #25 heard the Holy Prophet say, "***The Italians have our blood (The blood of the Moors) mixed in their veins, that is why they are so mean.***"

37. Bro. J. Foster Bey of Temple #4 and #25 heard the Holy Prophet say "***We (The Moors) are a hard head, stiff neck, mean set of people that have never did anything except at the point of a sword.***"

38. Bro. I. Cook Bey, Grand Governor of Illinois heard the Holy Prophet speak a parable. He said, "***I remember when I was on the soul plane. I remember when I was Noah. Noah was a carpenter, and he built the Ark. When the flood came, men came swimming out to the Ark, and knocked on the door, and said, 'Noah, Noah, let us in,' and I told them, 'The door is locked, and an angel came, and took the key away.'***"

39. Bro. I. Cook Bey. Grand Governor of Illinois told Bro. R. Love El, Grand Sheik of the M.S.T. of A. and Bro. C. Tyson Bey, Chairman of the M.S.T. of A. reported about the time, when the Holy Prophet Noble Drew Ali and Bro. C. Kirkman Bey went to the Pan American Conference in 1928. At that time, the Holy Prophet went there and represented the Moors, and there was an Indian Chief representing the American Indians. The Conference was in Havana, Cuba, and the nations of North, South and Central America were present. Former Secretary of State Hughes of the United States represented the United States at this conference. Bro. C. Kirkman Bey was the interpreter for the Holy Prophet at this conference. Bro. I. Cook Bey said that when the Holy Prophet and Bro. C. Kirkman Bey's ship was tied up at the dock, the Cuban army was standing on the dock, and Bro. Kirkman Bey

said something to them in Spanish, and the army came to attention, then he and the Holy Prophet came down from the ship. At the conference, Bro. C. Kirkman Bey addressed the conference in both Spanish and Arabic, and when the former Secretary of State of the United States, Charles Evans Hugh. heard Bro. Kirkman Bey speak, he said, "That's a dangerous man." Up to that period of time, the United States was operating off of an expired 50 year mandate for this land. At this conference, the mandate for this land was reportedly given to Prophet Noble Drew Ali. Bro. G. Cook Bey, Grand Sheik of Temple One reportedly said that "***Prophet Noble Drew Ali showed us the mandate in the Adept Chamber***."

40. Bro. I. Cook Bey, Grand Governor of IllInois, said that the Holy Prophet Noble Drew Ali told the Moors that "***The Europeans went to the Moroccan government, and asked for permission to come over here (to North America) to develop this land, and they were given a 50 year mandate to do so. Then the Europeans went to an old Sheik and asked him to give them some people to help them to develop this land. The Sheik told them to "Take those Moors, because they are not going to do anything."***"

41. Sister M. Lovett El, Grand Governor of Illinois said that the Holy Prophet Noble Drew Ali said, "***I had to go around my elbow to get to my thumb to get what I wanted established in this government.***"

42. Sister M. Howell Bey of Temple #19 said that the Holy Prophet Noble Drew Ali, while speaking would jump up in the air and laugh, and say "***Rome, 2000 years ago, you got me, but I got you today***."

43. Sister M. Lovett Bey, Grand Governor of Illinois said that the Holy Prophet Noble Drew Ali said, "***I placed a ball on Babylon, and it is rolling down, and anyone that gets in the way, is going to be ground to powder.***"

44. Bro. I. Cook Bey, Grand Governor of Illinois and other Moors said that the Holy Prophet said, "***You tore up everything that was brought to you, but I brought you something that you can't tear up. It will tear you up***."

45. Sister A. Brown El of Temple #4 and #25 said that the Holy Prophet Noble Drew Ali said, "***I am going to leave the European here, just long enough to teach you how to run a government.***"

46. Sister M. Tiggs El of Temple #9 said that the Holy Prophet said, "***I am going to repeat myself.***"

47. Bro. G. Cook Bey, Grand Sheik of Temple #1 said that the Holy Prophet said that "***If you have a dream and you forget what you dreamed, to remember it, place your forehead face down on your pillow, and you will remember it.***"

48. The Holy Prophet said, "***If you dream of me, it is like seeing me for true, because the devil cannot steal my appearance.***"

49. Bro. T. Booker Bey, Grand Natl. Treasurer said that when at a meeting where the Holy Prophet was present, he saw ten Arabians, five Turks, two Chinese, and one Japanese join the Moorish Science Temple of America, and the Secretary asked the Holy Prophet Noble Drew Ali, "Prophet, these people have got their nationality, what should I put on their Nationality Card?" The Prophet said "***The Moors were the first people, and all other people that use our name were adopted in to our tribe.***"

50. Bro, J. Foster Bey of Temple #4 and #25 said that he heard the Holy Prophet say "***People left the Garden of Eden, and died by the thousands, but it was the Moors that were able to traverse the desert, go into other parts of the world to inhabit.***"

51. Bro. J. Foster Bey of Temple #4 and #25 heard the Holy Prophet say, "***When the wild beast roamed the earth in large numbers, and you could hear the large birds flapping their wings at a long distance, it was the Moors that took the sword and went out and slayed the beast so that civilization could come in.***"

52. Sister M. Payton Bey of temple #4 and #25, and Bro. J. Davis Grand Governor of Michigan heard the Holy Prophet ask the Moors in Detroit, Michigan, "***How would you like to have your own Mayor and Chief of Police?***"

53. Bro. J. Foster Bey of Temple #4 and #25 said that the Holy Prophet said, "Before the End of Time, every knee will bow to Islam."

54. In the late 1920's, when there were thousands of Moors in the Moorish Science Temple of America, the Holy Prophet told the moors "***The membership is going to dwindle down to a handful, but keep the doors open, and I***

will drive the Asiatics in. " The Holy Prophet said, "***When I drive the Asiatics in, it's going to take 10 secretaries, just to write the names down.***"

55. Bro. J. Blakely Bey said the Holy Prophet said, "***When I raise my flood gate, it's going to take 16 secretaries to write down the names.***"

56. Bro. O. Payton Bey Grand Sheik of Branch Temple #25 (Ecorse, Michigan) said that the Holy Prophet said, "***Let all old business stay as it is, and all new business, do it in your free national name.***"

57. Sister A. Brown H of Temple #4 and #25 said that the Prophet told the Moors, "***Watch the newspapers and listen to the radio, I am going to make the European tell the truth.***"

58. Bro. J. Blakely Bey told the Moors that the Holy Prophet said that "***Things are going back to horse and buggy days.***"

59. Bro. B. Jones El, Assistant Grand Sheik of Temple #43 heard the Holy Prophet said, "***Children, one day, you are going to love me.***"

60. The Holy Prophet told the Moors, "***I am due in the East right now. I am going to have to go and straighten out the East, and then I will end up in the West. This (The West) will be the easiest. You will be able to be down and sleep, and wake up in peace. This will be, just a breakfast fight. By the time you eat breakfast, it will all be over with.***"

61. Bro. T. Booker Bey, Grand National Treasurer said the Holy Prophet said, "***One day, blood is going to flow in the streets up to a horse's brow.***"

62. The Holy Prophet said. "***One day, bombs are going to fall so that they won't miss a spot as wide as my shoe.***" He said that "***you are going to need a basement to hide in.***"

63. The Holy Prophet asked the Moors, "***How many of you can do something?***" (Some say that he was inquiring as to how many of them could work magic, etc.) Some of the Moors stood up. The Prophet pointed his finger at them, and said, "***I am going to kill you all.***"

64. The Holy Prophet Noble Drew Ali said, "***Don't worry about how you are going to be saved. It will be done in a conflict that cannot be told in words.***"

65. Sister M. Payton Bey of Temple #4 and #25 said that the Holy Prophet said, "***I got here, just in time.***" She said that the Europeans were looking for him with airplanes, and with dreadnoughts. When the Holy Prophet came into the country (The U.S.) He was asked, "Where are those books that you have?" She said that the Prophet just smiled, but He told the Moors that He had the book in His head. When the Holy Prophet dictated verses of the Holy Koran of the Moorish Science Temple of America to the printer, He did it from memory. The printer was amazed!

66. Sister M. Payton Bey of Temple #4 and #25 said that the Holy Prophet said, "***I have got the world in a jug, and the stopper in my hand.***" Others said that the Holy Prophet said, "***I have got the world in a jug, and the stopper in my hand. I have got the Asiatic, and I have got the European. I have got the silver and I have got the gold.***"

67. Bro. J. Blakely Bey said that the Holy Prophet said, "***It will take 50 years to find out what I brought you, and if you are not careful, 50 years after I am gone, you won't know that I have been here.***"

68. The Holy Prophet told the Moors, "***I brought you something that you can shout about.***"

69. Bro. G. Cook Bey, Grand Sheik of Temple #1 related that he set up a meeting of Christian preachers to meet with the Holy Prophet Noble Drew Ali to see whether these preachers would follow the Holy Prophet. Bro. G. Cook Bey had these ministers assembled, and he was addressing them before the Holy Prophet came to the meeting. One of the preachers said, "If He (speaking of the Holy Prophet) could do what Moses could, I would follow Him." The Holy Prophet was not present in the room when this statement was made, and the meeting place was on the third floor of the building that they were in. When the Holy Prophet arrived at the meeting, He told the preacher, "***I can do what Moses did, but if I came walking into the meeting with a lion on a chain, you would jump out of the window and kill yourself.***"

70. The Holy Prophet told the Moors "***Don't endanger your life with a fool.***"

71. Bro. J. Foster Bey of Temple #4 and #25 said that the Holy Prophet said, "***Before one jot or title of my word fail to come to pass, heaven and earth will pass away.***"

72. Bro. J. Blakely Bey said that the Holy Prophet said, "***There is going to be an earthquake that will split the United States in two.***"
73. Bro. E. Thomas El of Temple #4 and #43 said that the Holy Prophet said, "***One day, 50 pound hail stones are going to fall.***"
74. The Holy Prophet said, "***If my Principles are carried out (The Principles of Love, Truth, Peace, Freedom and Justice for our people in this land), the United States will be the richest and most prosperous country on the earth, if not, the worst is yet to come.***"
75. The Holy Prophet told the Moors, "***The times that have been, won't be no more.***"
76. The Holy Prophet let the Moors know that He was Jesus. He said, "***Those that were with me 2000 years ago, are with me today, and those that were against me 2000 years ago, are against me today.***"
77. Prophet Noble Drew Ali told the Moors, "***Moors, be yourself.***"
78. The Holy Prophet said, "***Moors, study yourself.***"
79. Sister Gaddy Bey of Tempe #4 and #25 said that the Holy Prophet said, "***Children, your hair is not kinky. It is woolly like your Brother Jesus.***"
80. Bro. T. Booker Bey. Grand National Treasurer said that the Holy Prophet said that "***The Moors were the off springs of Kings and Queens.***"
81. The Holy Prophet Noble Drew Ali said, "***Allah alone is perfect.***"
82. The Holy Prophet Noble Drew Ali said, "***Allah alone guides the destiny of the Moorish Science Temple of America.***"
83. Sister M. Howell Bey of Temple #19 said that the Holy Prophet said that when the Europeans asked him, "Will we be saved this time?" The Holy Prophet said, "***If you do, it will be through the Moors.***"
84. The Holy Prophet told the Moors that "***The Europeans were not going to give up until he looked death in the face.***"
85. Bro. J. Blakely Bey told the Moors that the Holy Prophet said, "***It doesn't make any difference which way things look like they are going, it's all going to end up in the Asiatics hands.***"

86. The Holy Prophet Noble Drew Ali told the Moors, "***Children, when you get on top, treat the European nice.***"

87. Sister M. Payton Bey of Temple #4 and #25 said that the Holy Prophet said, "***Let your good deeds out number your bad deeds, and when you pass away, you won't have anything to worry about.***"

88. Sister M. Payton Bey said that the Holy Prophet told the Moors, "***I have got spies everywhere.***"

89. Bro. J. Blakely Bey said that the Holy Prophet told the Moors, "***Not throw away your slave names (your family last name), because we have a birth right under them. For the work that our ancestors did in slavery time, we will be paid off for this, and with compounded interest.***"

90. The Holy Prophet told the Moors to "***Get a good European education, and I can use you.***"

91. Sister M. Payton Bey said that the Holy Prophet said, "***The biggest fool is the educated fool.***"

92. Bro. O. Payton Bey of temple #4 and #25 said that the Holy Prophet said, "***Moors should learn Spanish as a second language.***"

93. Bro. W. Davis El, Grand Governor of Michigan said that the Holy Prophet said, "***Don't even carry a pocket knife.***"

94. Bro. J. Brown El of Temple #25 said that the Holy Prophet said, "***One day, people are going to be so hungry that the only way that you will be able to turn them away, will be at the point of a gun.***"

95. Bro. J. Blakely Bey said that the Holy Prophet said, "***The third and fourth generation will see the good of my work.***"

96. Sister A. Brown El of Temple #4 and #25 said that the Holy Prophet told the Moors, "***Take a good look at me, so that you will know me when you see me.***" She also said that the Holy Prophet said, "***When you see me don't speak to me unless I speak to you first.***"

97. Bro. Smith Bey of Temple #3 and #9 stated that some Asiatics paid some hit men to kill the Holy Prophet. When the hit men went to the temple where the Holy Prophet was teaching, that they opened the door, and found the

temple building full of soldiers. The hit men went back to the people that hired them, and told them, "Don't you pay us to do anything to any of those Moorish Americans."

98. Bro. T. Booker Bey, Grand National Chairman said that the Holy Prophet gave a party for the Moors, and that the Prophet had everything fixed up nice. He even had pool tables for their enjoyment. The Moors were happy, and the Holy Prophet said, "***I am happy, when my Moors are happy.***" But some unconscious Asiatics tried to break up the party. When they tried, some of the Moors, who were members of the National Guard, went to the Armory, and came back to the party with army tanks, trucks, and guns. When the Asiatics saw this, they took off with such fright that some of them ran into buildings, and knocked themselves out. He said that the word got out, "Don't mess with Prophet Noble Drew Ali, because He is connected with the government."

99. Bro. Blakely Bey said that the Holy Prophet told the Moors, "***Don't name your children Ali.***"

100. Bro. J. Foster Bey of Temple #4 and #25 told the Moors that the Holy Prophet said. "***When the Moors ruled Spain, we had street lights in Seville, Spain 400 years before they had them anywhere else in Europe.***"

101. Bro. T. Booker Bey. Grand National Treasurer said that he was walking down the street in Chicago, Illinois, and an Arabian came out of a store, and asked him to come into the store. He went with him. The Arabian pointed at a man, and asked him. "Do you know who this is?" Bro. Booker Bey said, "That is my Prophet." The Holy Prophet said, "***All right son.***" The store was full of Arabians, and Bro. T. Booker Bey said that all of them had Nationality Cards for the Moorish Science Temple of America.

102. Moors that were in the Temple during the lifetime of the Holy Prophet Noble Drew Ali said that when the Holy Prophet came to town, you would have to go to the temple early to get a seat, and you could not get a seat in the front row because the foreign Moslems would be sitting in the front row to see and hear the Holy Prophet.

103. The Holy Prophet Noble Drew Ali use to heal people, and people came to him for counsel. Bro. G. Cook Bey, Grand Sheik of Temple #1 said that when he was in Baltimore, MD. the Holy Prophet was healing people. Bro. G. Cook

Bey went to the head of the stairs, and told the people, "The Prophet is tired He has been healing people all day long Go home."

104. Sister E. Sims El of Temple #4 and #43 said that she went to the Holy Prophet, because she had been sick. The Holy Prophet listened to her, and said, "***Sister, you are going to get well.***" But that is as much of that meeting that she related, but her husband, Bro. R. Sims El, Grand Sheik of Temple #4 said that the Holy Prophet said to her also, "***Sister, go to the Temple, if you have got to crawl.***"

105. Sister A. Brown El of Temple #4 and #25 said that the Holy Prophet said in the 1920S, "***Some of my best Moors are still in the church.***"

106. 106. Bro. O. Payton Bey of Temple #4 and #25 said that the Holy Prophet said, "***There are going to be new Moors that are going to come in with their eyes wide open, seeing and knowing, that are going to take you old Moors, seat you in the back, and carry out my law.***"

107. Bro. J. Blakely Bey said that the Holy Prophet told the Moors, "***Moslems are not made, they are born.***"

108. Bro. J. Foster Bey of Temple #4 and #25 told the Moors that the Holy Prophet said, "***I can throw out a spirit that would make the Moors want to fight, and then throw out another spirit that would bring them back to peace.***"

109. Bro. T. Booker Bey, Grand National Treasurer said at one night's temple meeting, a dirty Moor tried to attack the Holy Prophet with a knife. The Moors in attendance just stood there. After the event, the Holy Prophet told the Moors, "***I have got a good mind to leave you.***" Bro. T. Booker Bey said that the Moors got down on their knees, and begged the Prophet not to leave them. After their begging the Holy Prophet not to leave, a man appeared in the room that looked like a Turk, and he said, "If you harm a hair of his head (speaking of the Holy Prophet) we will come and destroy you all."

110. Sister A. Brown El of Temple #4 and #25 said that the Holy Prophet told the Moors that "***The climate was going to change. The cold weather will be in the South, and the warm weather will be in the North.***"

111. Bro. T. Booker Bey, Grand National Treasurer Grand National Treasurer said that the Holy Prophet said, "***I like good peas and beans. I am going to save 8% of the Europeans, because they are good farmers.***"

112. Sister A. Brown and Bro. C. Barker Bey said that the Holy Prophet told the Moors, "***Don't let none of those foreign Moslems get up in your rostrum.***"

113. Sister M. Tiggs El of Temple #9 said that the Holy Prophet said, "***One day, you are going to smell the Europeans before you see them, in boxcars, going back to Europe.***"

114. The Holy Prophet said. "***If you steal my money, it's going to burn up in your pocket.***"

115. Bro. J. Gill Bey of Temple #4 and #25 and the Moorish Home Office #1 said the Holy Prophet said. "***If you have money, and don't give it to me (to help out in the divine and national movement of the M.S.T. of A.), I am going to get it anyway.***"

116. The Holy Prophet told the Moors that "***One day, there are going to be so few people, that when you see an old Moor, you will run up to him, and kiss him all on top of his head.***"

117. The Holy Prophet told the Moors that "***There will be so few men, that a child will go to the store, and return home, and tell his mother, 'Mother, I saw a man.'***"

118. Sister M. Howell El of Temple #19 said that the Holy Prophet pointed his finger, and said, "***My sheep know the sound of my voice; a stranger will not follow.***"

119. Sister M. Howell El of Temple #19 said that the Holy Prophet told the Moors, "***I brought you your nationality, your religion, and title to your vast estate. What do you want me to do; kill you?***"

120. Bro. G. Cook Bey, Grand Sheik of Temple 1 said the Holy Prophet said, "***While I am talking to you Moors, my spirit is over in India with them, and those old sisters are jumping this high (They were jumping as high as He was holding his hand), because of my coming to them.***"

121. Sister M. Howell El said that the Holy Prophet told the Moors, "***I am going to burn up sin, both root and branch.***"

122. Sister M. Howell El said that Bro. C. Kirkman Bey told her that the Holy Prophet said, "***Anytime a Moslem goes into a church for any reason; it ceases to be church, and it is a temple.***"

123. Sister M. Howell El said that the Holy Prophet said, "***You can walk down the street by yourself now, but one day, you won't be able to do that.***"

124. Bro. I. Cook Bey, Grand Governor of Illinois said that the Holy Prophet said, "***I have got two wives. One day, you will be able to have two, or as many as you can afford.***"

125. Bro. O. Payton Bey of Temple #4 and #25 said that the Holy Prophet told the Moors, "***I am going to let the fire touch some of you old Moors' shirt tail.***"

126. Bro. T. Booker Bey, Grand National Treasurer said that the Holy Prophet told the Moors "***I am going to let the fire scorch some of my good Moors.***"

127. Bro. E. Thomas El of Temple #43 said the Holy Prophet said, "***Money will be burnt in the streets, and we won't be able to buy much; and when I put my spirit in the streets, you won't be able to sell your car for 25 cents.***"

128. Bro. E. Thomas said that the Holy Prophet said, "***The European will seek peace, but none shall be found.***"

129. Bro. E. Thomas El said that the Holy Prophet said, "***All nations will turn against the United States, one day.***"

130. The Holy Prophet said, "***One day, the United States will not be able to do any business, unless they do it through the Asiatics.***"

131. Sister M. Howell Bey of Temple #19 said that the Holy Prophet said, "***I am going to stop the Europeans from thinking if two or three of them get together on something, they will go back, and tear it up.***"

132. During the time of the Holy Prophet, one of the Sisters in Chicago, Illinois was living loosely, and going in the alley to so act with her turban on. The Holy Prophet told the Moors, "***Stay out of the alley with your turbans on.***"

133. Bro. J. Foster Bey of Temple #4 and #25 told the Moors that the Holy Prophet told the Moors in Detroit,

Michigan to "***Carry your fez to the temple.***" This was supposedly said because some Moors were wearing their fezzes in bars and other places of ill repute.

134. Bro. J. Blakely Bey told the Moors that the Holy Prophet told the Moors, "***People are going to be dying like hogs with the cholera, and the doctors won't know what is wrong with them. The only thing that is going to save them is my remedies.***"
135. Sister M. Lovett El Grand Governor of Illinois said that the Holy Prophet said, "***My remedies will cure you of anything that you weren't born with.***"
136. Bro. J. Blakely Bey said that the Holy Prophet said that "***We are going to be taxed to death.***"
137. Bro. J. Blakely Bey told the Moors that the Holy Prophet said, "***Atlantis is going to arise again.***"
138. J. Blakely Bey told the Moors that the Holy Prophet said, "***If you are not careful, your own brothers will try to put you in slavery.***"
139. Bro. J. Blakely Bey told the Moors that the Holy Prophet said, "***If you don't leave here right with me this time, you won't make it back here in human form.***"
140. Sister A. Brown El of Temple #4 and #25 said that the Holy Prophet said, "***One day, some of you Moors are going to be walking around with skippers (maggots) falling out of you, praying to die, and won't be able to die.***"
141. Sister A. Brown El said that the Holy Prophet said, "***Moors look your best.***"
142. Sister M Payton Bey of Temple #4 and #25 said that the Holy Prophet said, "***Try to have your temples in buildings, where the meetings are on the second floor.***"
143. Bro. O. Payton Bey of Temple #4 and #25 said that the Holy Prophet said, "***I took the cover off all the secret organizations.***"
144. The Holy Prophet said, "***Imitate I, The Prophet.***" And He said, "***Moorish Leaders, live a life of love, so that you will be loved as I the Prophet is loved.***"
145. Sister M. Tiggs El said that the Holy Prophet said that "***At the End of time, those that will be in the apparatus will be able to look down on earth, see people that you***

know, fleeing for their life."

146. The Holy Prophet told the Moors that "***They sleep too much***".

147. Bro. I. Cook Bey, Grand Governor of Illinois said that the Holy Prophet told the Moors, "***Children, sow good seeds.***"

148. Sister, M. Payton Bey, Grand National Treasurer said that the Holy Prophet said, "***You are from Missouri, I have got to show you.***"

149. Bro. T. Booker Bey, Grand National Treasurer said that the Holy Prophet told the Moors, "***In two weeks, I am going down South. When I get down there, the Ku Klux Klan is going to stop me. At first, it is going to look like they are against me. Then they are going to lead me where I am going.***"

150. Bro. I. Cook Bey, Grand Governor of Illinois said that the Holy Prophet said, "***If you doubt that I am a prophet, watch my prophecies.***"

151. The Holy Prophet told the Moors, "***You are going to be saved in a conflict that cannot be told in words***."

152. Sister A. Brown El of Temple #4 and #25 said that the Holy Prophet said, "***Don't throw away your Bibles, because I am going to use them to condemn the government.***"

153. The Holy Prophet said, "***This is the uniting of Asia.***"

154. Bro. G. Cook Bey, Grand Sheik of Temple #1 said that he asked the Holy Prophet to tell him about a particular star in the heavens, and the Holy Prophet told him," ***If you go and get 10 people, I will tell you about that star.***" Bro. Cook Bey said that he could not get anyone, and he returned to the Holy Prophet, and informed him of that. The Holy Prophet told him, "***I could tell you some things that would turn your brain to water.***"

155. Bro. I Cook Bey, Grand Governor of Illinois, said that the Holy Prophet said, "***You can lead a horse to water, but you can't make him drink. I am going to lead some of you Moors all the way up to salvation, and you are going to turn around and go the other way.***"

156. Bro. I. Cook Bey said that the Holy Prophet said, "***I am a General as well as a Prophet.***" "***I was Mohammed. Mohammed defeated the Roman Empire. When I conquered Rome, we went in with the sword. You***

could hear the swords swinging. I cut the head of Rome off; pulled down the flags; sent letters to the other European governments, and asked them was I right. They said, "Yes Mohammed, you are right. Just let us have a place to live." The Holy Prophet said, "I went into Rome with 72,000 men. When I ran out or men, I reached down, and picked up a hand full of sand, I threw it up in the air, and when it came down, there were soldiers seated on camels."

157. Bro. I. Cook Bey said that the Holy Prophet said, "The ***only thing that would surprise me, is if a Moor would do right.***"

158. Bro. I. Cook Bey said that the Holy Prophet said, "***One day, you are going to look for the good Moors, and you won't be able to find them.***"

159. Sister A. Brown El of Temple #4 and #25 said the Holy Prophet said, "***Your Nationality Card is going to change on you in your pocket.***"

160. The Holy Prophet said, "I ***am not going to wake up all the Asiatics at once, because they may tear up something.***"

161. The Holy Prophet said, "***If my own mother is not right, I am not going to let her get by.***"

162. The Holy Prophet said, "***Pray you don't have to make your flight in the winter time.***"

163. Bro. J. Foster Bey of Temple #4 and #25 said that the Holy Prophet said, "***If you put your hand to the gospel plow and turn loose, it would be better, if you never took hold.***"

164. The Holy Prophet said, "***Woe upon the one that scatters my flock.***"

165. The Holy Prophet said, "***Woe upon the man that calls himself a Jew.***"

166. The Holy Prophet said, "***One day you will see a $20.00 bill in the street, and would not bend over to pick it up.***"

167. Bro. G. Cook Bey, Grand Sheik of Temple #1 said that the Holy Prophet Noble Drew Ali said, "***One day, you are going to look out into the streets, and the streets are going to be filled with men with turbans and fezzes, and the highways are going to be blocked.***"

168. The Holy Prophet said, "***A good Moorish leader must***

study his Holy Koran and Divine Constitution and By laws."

169. Sister M. Tiggs El of Temple #9 said that the Holy Prophet said, "***Cats are evil spirits, and if you knew what a black cat was, you would not want one around.***"

170. Sister M. Tiggs El of Temple #9 said that the Holy Prophet said, "***Don't keep dogs in your house, because if you inhale one of its hairs, it could cut your throat.***"

171. Sister M. Tiggs El of Temple #9 said the Holy Prophet said, "***You say that you want some pure meat to eat, no one is going to kill a camel for you to eat over here.***"

172. Sister M. Tiggs El of Temple #9 said that the Holy Prophet said, "***The Moors watchdog is not a dog, but an elephant.***"

173. The Holy Prophet told the Moors, "***When children start crying in a meeting, take them out of the meeting.***"

174. Bro. G. Cook Bey, Grand Sheik of Temple One said that the Holy Prophet Noble Drew Ali said, "***I am going to save you all, if I have got to kill you all.***"

175. Bro. I. Cook Bey, Grand Governor of Illinois said that the Holy Prophet Noble Drew Ali said, "***If I cannot teach you here, I will teach you on the soul plane.***"

176. Sister M. Howell Bey of Temple #19 said that the Holy Prophet said, "***This food here is just European poison.***"

177. Bro. I. Cook Bey, Grand Governor of Illinois said that the Holy Prophet said, "***When I was born, it turned black dark in the day time. The people put their hoes down, and came out of the fields.***"

178. Sister M. Lovett El, Grand Governor of Illinois said that the Holy Prophet asked her, "***Do you have anyone in your temple that can speak foreign languages?***" She said yes. At that time, she was the Grand Sheikess of Temple #9. She said that one cold night that she took Bro. C. Kirkman Bey to the Holy Prophet's office, where she said, "Brother Prophet, this is the Brother that I was talking about" she said, "I thought that I was introducing him to the Prophet, but they already knew each other, because they had went to school together." She said that the Holy Prophet asked Bro. C. Kirkman Bey, "***Can you speak high German?***" Bro. C. Kirkman Bey said, "Yes, but I am a little

rusty." She said that the Holy Prophet reached in to a trunk pulled out a book, and dusted it off with a feather duster, and handed it to Bro. Kirkman Bey, and he read from it. The Holy Prophet was satisfied, and told him that He had to go down to Cuba, and He wanted him to go with Him. Bro. C. Kirkman Bey told the Prophet that he had a wife and a child or children. The Holy Prophet let him know that they would be provided for.

179. Before the bank crash in 1929, Sister A. Brown El of Temple #4 and #25 said that the Holy Prophet told the Moors, "***If you have money in the bank, get it out.***" Some said that the Prophet told the Moors to put their money in the post office. Those that obeyed the Holy Prophet saved their money, and those that did not, lost their money. Bro. C. Carriton Bey Grand Governor of New York said that one day he was at the annual national convention, and Bro. C. Kirkman Bey sent for him to come outside to witness something. There was a European man, his wife, and daughter there. The European man asked Bro. C. Kirkman Bey "Where is that little man that used to be around." Bro. C. Kirkman Bey let them know that he was no longer with us. These Europeans started crying. They were looking for the Holy Prophet. That man was able to save his money during the bank crash, because he obeyed the Holy Prophet, and took his money out of the bank.

180. The Holy Prophet told the Brothers to "***Use kind words toward your wife.***"

181. Bro. J. Foster Bey of Temple #4 and #25 said that the Holy Prophet Noble Drew Ali said, "***A beggar nation cannot attain to its highest degree of spirituality.***"

182. Sister M. Lovett El, Grand Governor of Illinois said that the Holy Prophet said, "***One day, men are going to be running so fast that their coat tails will be standing straight out. You will be able to shoot dice on their coat tails. They are going to be running to get into the Temple. The last ones to make it into the temple will be the preachers, and the Europeans are going to be beating them over the head, driving them in.***"

183. The Holy Prophet said, "***I am going to make the European enforce my law.***"

184. Bro. T. Booker Bey, Grand Natl. Treasurer said that the

Holy Prophet said, "***The Moors were living up and down the Mississippi river before the European man came here.***"

185. The Holy Prophet told the Moors "***That we need to have warehouses.***"

186. The Holy Prophet said, "***Moorish leaders, don't burden my Moors.***"

187. Bro. O. Payton Bey of Temple #4 and #25 said that the Holy Prophet said, "***When you take care of Temple business go in numbers of two, three, five, and seven.***"

188. Sister M. Payton Bey of Temple #4 and #25 said the Holy Prophet said, "***Everyone needs to have a secret.***"

189. Bro. I. Foster Bey, Bro. W. Davis El, Grand Governor of Michigan, and Bro. J. Blakely Bey, who were all members of Temple 4 in Detroit, Michigan during the lifetime of the Holy Prophet, all said that at one meeting, when the Holy Prophet was in Detroit speaking in the Temple, an Asiatic got up while the Holy Prophet was speaking and said, "If that man is a prophet, I would be willing to give up my life." This angered some of the Moors that heard it. Bro. W. Davis El said that some of the Moors started moving up on this man with their hands in their pockets, and they were going to cut him to death, but the Holy Prophet held up his hand, and said, "***Children, did you hear that? It is too bad.***" After the Holy Prophet spoke those words, this Asiatic fell back into his seat, and slumped down. When the meeting was over, the Moors carried him out of the building, he was dead.

190. Sister A, Brown El of Temple #4 and #25 said that the Holy Prophet said, "***If your Brother does something wrong to you, don't call him a "nigger." Call him a dirty Moor.***"

191. Bro. Smith Bey of Temple #3 and #9 said that the Holy Prophet Noble Drew Ali said, "***Boys, why don't you be like I, your Prophet. I don't drink, and I don't smoke, but if you do, don't stop it all at once. If you do, you may hurt something.***"

192. Sister M. Payton Bey of Temple #4 and #25 said that the Holy Prophet said, "***Don't drink and come to the temple, and sit down next to people with liquor on your breath.***"

193. Sister M. Payton Bey said that the Holy Prophet said, "***If you just have to drink, go into your room.***"

194. Sister M. Payton Bey said that the Holy Prophet said, "***If it were not for that little piece of red flannel, we would not get into so much trouble.***"

195. Sister M. Payton Bey said that the Holy Prophet said, "***The only thing that hurts a duck is his bill.***"

196. Sister M, Lovett El, Grand Governor of Illinois said that the Holy Prophet said, "***If I were you, I would get ready before you are made to do so.***"

197. Bro. O. Payton Bey of Temple #4 and #25 said that the Holy Prophet said, "***One day, the United States will not be able to do any business, unless they do it through the Asiatic.***"

198. Bro. I. Cook Bey, Grand Governor said that the Holy Prophet said "***Children, if you want to come up to see me, you can.***"

199. The Holy Prophet Noble Drew All said, "I ***come to set you free from that state of mental slavery that I found you in.***"

200. Bro. J. Blakely Bey said that the Holy Prophet said, "***Don't put the European on your brother.***"

201. Sister A. Brown El of Temple #4 and #25 said that the Holy Prophet Noble Drew Ali said, "***If you go to an Adept Meeting, don't tell anyone who does not go, what happened at the meeting.***" (

202. The Holy Prophet said, "***A Moorish leader is not to get up to speak under the influence of liquor, or any harmful motive that will seek to break up the families of men.***"

203. Bro. O. Payton Bey of Temple #4 and #25 said that the Holy Prophet Noble Drew Ali said, "***If you have a wife, and she does not belong to the Temple, instead of giving her one apple, give her two.***"

204. Bro. O. Payton Bey of Temple #4 and #25 said that the Holy Prophet said, "***If someone assaults you, flee from him. If you cannot flee from him, turn around, and drop the world on him.***"

205. Bro. J. Blakely Bey said that the Holy Prophet said, "If ***you don't leave here right with me this time, you won't make it back here in human form.***"

206. At the first National Moorish Science Temple of America convention, the Holy Prophet Noble Drew Ali said "***The garment that I have on represents power and if you obey my voice, you will have power with me. I am going to free you, though it's hard, because of your mixture, which brings about many different spirits. When you fail to hear my voice, you are lost. It is against the law to stand up in any audience intoxicated. The leader is not to stay out all night, giving earnings away to someone else. You who are heads of Temples, it is easy for you to destroy the influence of the Temple; now lace up your shoes, and get right. You, stop figuring out your way, how your salvation shall come, just follow me. You can say one thing Moors, you have made a start for the kingdom. If you want success, you must follow the Prophet. Husbands take care of your wives, and families. Wives keep your homes and children clean. I have done more than you think. I want you to help me by your good deeds of living at home, and abroad. It is through your good, not with your lips, trying to be the front seat in everything, always standing in my face. Moors, be careful of your steps, leaders of Temples must be careful how they walk. They must be an example.***" The Holy Prophet said "***I am not asleep; it will take you Moors a long time to find out what I did today. When you all go home, don't start no stuff, for I will be right there listening at you.***" The Holy Prophet Noble Drew Ali also said, "***This is no social organization, it is a divine and national movement. By you being born here doesn't make you a citizen.***" "***Look what I have on, now this was handed to me by the government. It represents the royal prince.***"

207. Sister M. Whitehead El cited the Holy Prophet in 1928 as saying, "***I have mended the broken wires, and have connected them with the higher powers.***"

208. The Holy Prophet Noble Drew Ali said, "The ***times that have been, won't be no more.***"

209. Sister A. Brown El of Temple #4 and #25 said that the Holy Prophet said, "***Some of you Moors are going to throw away your name, just for a morsel of bread.***"

210. Sister M. Washington El of Temple #43 said that the Holy Prophet said. "***One day, there is going to be a holy war.***"

211. The Holy Prophet Noble Drew Ali said, "***There is but one Allah, one Prophet of the Temple, and one Moorish Science Temple of America.***"

212. The Holy Prophet told the Moors, "I ***have come, and taken away all the excuses.***"

213. Bro. J. Gill Bey of Temple #4 and the colony in Prince George, VA., said that the Holy Prophet said, "***I forgive you of everything that you did before I came, you are responsible for your deeds now.***"

214. Sister M. Payton Bey of Temple #4 and #25 said that the Holy Prophet said, "***If I tell you that I am going to do a thing, I have done it already***."

215. Sister M. Payton Bey said that the Holy Prophet said, "***I have fixed everything; I have stopped up every rat hole.***"

216. The Holy Prophet Noble Drew Ali, "***I have come for the children, and the unborn generations.***"

217. Bro. I. Cook Bey, Illinois of Illinois said that the Holy Prophet said, "***There is going to be famine in the land.***"

218. The Holy Prophet Noble Drew Ali said, "***Chicago is going to be your new Mecca.***"

219. Bro. G. Cook Bey, Grand Sheik of Temple 1 said that the Holy Prophet Noble Drew Ali said, "The ***only one that works all the time, is a coolie.***"

220. Bro. J. Blakely Bey said that the Holy Prophet Noble Drew Ali said that "***The Grand Sheik of a Temple should go to the Temple, hang the Charter on the wall, say the Moorish American prayer, when it is time for the meeting to open, and if no one comes to the meeting after he sits and waits for one and half hours, then take the Charter down off the wall and go home.***"

221. Sister M. Payton Bey of Temple #4 and #25 said that the Holy Prophet said, "***Before the End of Time, I am going to lower down the evil spirits, and let them incarnate.***"

222. Bro. J. Blakely Bey said that the Holy Prophet said, "I ***would like to save half of the people, but I am going to try to save a fourth of the people.***" "***There is just going to be a handful saved. I can count them on my fingers,***

and have fingers left over".

223. The Holy Prophet said, "***One day, all of the property is going back to the government.***"

224. Sister A. Brown El of Temple #4 and #25 said that the Holy Prophet said, "***Boil your drinking water.***"

225. Bro. J. Foster Bey while the Assistant Grand Sheik of Temple 25 told the Moors that the Holy Prophet told the Moors after a meeting, and most of the people had gone home, "*Wake up you sleepy headed Moors. I am going to* ***take you up above the sun, moon and stars, around the throne of the Mighty Allah.***" Bro. J. Foster Bey said that the Holy Prophet took them up above the blue ethers, around the throne of Allah. This happened in Detroit, Michigan in the late 1920's. Bro. J. Foster Bey concluded with the words, "Moors, your Prophet was a Prophet."

226. Bro. T. Booker Bey, Grand National Treasurer, said that the Holy Prophet Noble Drew Ali said, "***I have got the Romans in the palm of my hand.***"

227. Bro. T. Booker Bey, Grand National Treasurer said that the Holy Prophet said, "***The Moors are a dangerous people. I am not going to wake you all up at once; if I do, I won't be able to do anything with you myself.***"

228. Sister M. Lovett El, Grand Governess, said that the Holy Prophet said, "***One day, there are going to be so many women, a man is going to have to run for his life.***"

229. Bro. T. Booker Bey, Grand National Treasurer said that the Holy Prophet Noble Drew Ali said, "***The Moors once ruled the world; now get ready to rule it again. But this time it's going to be done under Love, Truth, Peace, Freedom and Justice.***"

230. Bro. I. Cook Bey, Grand Governor of Illinois said that the Holy Prophet said, "***I can do what Jesus did, but you are not in the condition that those people were in.***"

231. Bro. J. Foster Bey of Temple #4 and #25 said that the Holy Prophet said, "***The European is our fellow man.***"

232. The Prophet said, "***Money does not make the man, and clothes do not make the man. It is character and free national standards that make the man.***"

233. Bro. O. Payton Bey, Grand Sheik of Branch Temple #25 (Ecorse, M.I.) said that the Holy Prophet said, "***If you try to***

tell what a man is by looking at him, you are burnt up from the start."

234. Bro. J. Foster Bey of Temple #4 and #25 said that the Holy Prophet said, "***If your brother wants something, give it to him so that he won't sin.***"

235. The Holy Prophet said, "***I am the fifth, and last Prophet, and I am five times more powerful than I was before.***"

236. The Holy Prophet told The Moors "***If you want European Grand Sheiks, I can give them to you.***"

237. During the First Annual National Convention in 1928, one of the Grand Governors of a State failed to appear at the Convention. Bro. J. Blakely Bey said that the Holy Prophet sent the Grand Governor a telegram informing him, that if he did not attend the Convention, that He (The Holy Prophet) was going to have the federal agents to arrest him.

238. The Holy Prophet told the Moors, "***When you get married, go before your Grand Sheik, and let him perform the ceremony***". Some of the Moors did not obey The Holy Prophet's order, so He told the Moors, "***Go downtown, and buy your wives from the Europeans.***"

239. Sis. Whitehead El stated that the Holy Prophet said "***The garment I have on represents power and if you obey my voice you will have power with me. I am going to free you though it's hard because of your mixture which brings about many different spirits. When you fail to hear my voice you are lost. It is against the law to stand up in any audience intoxicated. The leader is not to stay out all night giving earnings away to someone else. You, who are heads of Temples, it is easy for you to destroy the influence of the Temple and me. Now lace up your shoes and get right!***" Sis. Whitehead El stated that the Holy Prophet said "***Our nationality in this government began with the parade.***" Sis. Whitehead El stated the Holy Prophet said "***This is not no social organization it is a Divine and National Movement. By you being born here don't make you a citizen. Look what I have on, now this was handed to me by the government. It represents the Royal Prince.***"

240. Bro. J. Blakely Bey stated that the Holy Prophet said "***Above all Moors, don't put the European on your brothers.***"

241. Bro. J. Blakely Bey stated that the Holy Prophet said "***Don't***

try to deal out justice, for justice belongs to Allah, and Allah alone."

242. Bro. J. Blakely Bey stated that the Holy Prophet said "***Moors, it will take you ten years to know what is on your nationality card, and you will be eighteen years understanding what I have come for and what I have done.***"

243. Bro. J. Blakely Bey stated that the Holy Prophet said "***Moors don't worry about the south, for I will take care of the south***.

244. Bro. J. Blakely Bey stated that the Holy Prophet said "***Don't think that a fez or a turban on your head makes you a Moslem, Moslems are born, not made.***"

245. Bro. J. Blakely Bey stated that the Holy Prophet said "***Islam can draw you or it can drive you, and Islam can save you or it can destroy you.***"

246. Bro. J. Blakely Bey stated that the Holy Prophet said "***I am going to drive the Moors back home to Islam if I have to cut their bread off.***"

247. Bro. J. Blakely Bey stated that the Holy Prophet said "***Many of you who think you are running away from the Prophet don't know that the further you run away from me, the closer you are coming to me, and when you wind up running you will be right in my arms.***"

248. Bro. J. Blakely Bey stated that the Holy Prophet said "***The Moorish Science Temple of America is like a wheel in a wheel turning, when I came the wheel was turning west, but since I have come I have started it to turning back east.***"

249. Bro. J. Blakely Bey stated that the Holy Prophet said "***Celebrate my birthday January the 8th, invite your Asiatic friends to come out and enjoy it with you. Yes, bring out your baskets of food to the Temple and banquet them.***"

250. Bro. J. Blakely Bey stated that the Holy Prophet said "***These Verbal Laws are Everlasting and Eternal just as much as my Written Laws.***"

251. Bro. Edward Mealy El, Supreme Grand Sheik, stated that the Holy Prophet said "***Make yourself perfect upon all subject matters that you may act intelligent on all lines of procedures.***"

252. The Holy Prophet once stated that "***The grand body shall make the laws and the supreme council shall interpret the laws and be the sole judges of what constitute a violation of the laws that are made.***"

253. Bro. Edward Mealy El stated that the Holy Prophet said "***I have my number, and my work of redeeming you people is finished, and I must now go, or I can't return; and if I don't return, I can't deliver you, and if I don't deliver you, then my coming is in vain.***"

254. It is stated by a Moor that He (the Prophet) told the people in Chicago that he was a prophet and to prove it he said the star and crescent would appear together in the heavens on December 19th 1925. It did.

255. Bro. Edward Mealy El stated that the Holy prophet told him "***You do what I tell you, never mind what they say, I have given you Law, Koran, and Constitution, and I expect you to enforce my Law and do I say, never mind what 'they' say or do. 'They' can do nothing but die.***"

256. Bro. Edward Mealy El stated that The Holy Prophet told him "***Children, there won't be but a few saved; because you are not going to do what I tell you. You way you want, and your way you are going to have. But your way leads downward Children; so you better do like I tell you. If you do like I tell you, there is a chance for you, if not; there is nothing for you, but death.***"

257. The Holy Prophet said "***They will take this movement down so low; it will disappear from the face of the earth.***"

258. The Prophet said "***Hold me up and I will draw all men unto you.***"

259. The Prophet was quoted as saying "***Asiatic Preachers and Masons will be the last to come home. They will fight me tooth and claw but cannot win.***"

Additional Notes

Califa Media™

A Moorish Guide Publishing Company

califamedia.com

Also Available From Califa Media

77 Amazing Facts About the Moors

Moorish Children's Guide to History and Culture

Moorish Jewels Series

Moors in America: A Compilation

Moslem Girls' Training Guide a.k.a. The Sisters' Auxiliary Handbook

Nationality, the Order of the Day

Noble Drew Ali Plenipotentiaries

Official Proclamation of Real Moorish American Nationality

Well, Come to Klanada

Who Stole the Fez, Moors or Shriners?

Other Volumes in the Califa Uhuru Series

Vol. 1: Holy Koran of the Moorish Holy Temple of Science, Circle 7

Vol. 2: "I'm Going to Repeat Myself." : A Collection of Artifacts Authored by Noble Prophet Drew Ali and the M.S.T. of A.

Vol. 3: Mysteries of the Silent Brotherhood of the East a.ka. The Red Book, a.k.a. Sincerity

www.ingramcontent.com/pod-product-compliance
Lightning Source LLC
Chambersburg PA
CBHW050526190726
48284CB00003B/959